MORE THAN LUCKY

Knowing that Patty was facing the loss of her home, Danny offered his house in the rear for her and her children. The two took a liking to each other and had frequent heart-to-heart chats. A bold and candid person, Patty often talked to Danny about the path he had chosen in life.

"I knew when I was fourteen I didn't want a regular job. I wanted excitement and wanted people to know who I was, to respect me. But I also wanted them to know that I have a good side despite what I do."

Patty even rebuked Danny for the danger he lived with.

"How can you go through life always having to look over your shoulder?"

"Hey, I'm Irish Catholic. I've got the best guardian angel there is," Danny replied. "Besides, the man upstairs pulls the strings. I'm not going anywhere until He says so."

"Do you think you're going to get to heaven because of all the money that you give away?" Patty asked candidly.

Danny laughed and shook his head.

"Boy, the things you come up with," he said. "That's what I like about you. Now, don't you know that all us Irish people go to heaven?"

KILL THE IRISHMAN

"A terrific read."

—*The Book Reader*

KILL THE IRISHMAN

THE WAR THAT CRIPPLED THE MAFIA

RICK PORRELLO

POCKET BOOKS

New York   London   Toronto   Sydney

Pocket Books
A Division of Simon & Schuster, Inc.
1230 Avenue of the Americas
New York, NY 10020

Copyright © 1998, 2001, 2004, 2006, 2011 by Rick Porrello

Prior editions published by Next Hat Press

All rights reserved, including the right to reproduce this book or portions thereof in any form whatsoever. For information address Pocket Books Subsidiary Rights Department, 1230 Avenue of the Americas, New York, NY 10020

First Pocket Books paperback edition March 2011

POCKET and colophon are registered trademarks of Simon & Schuster, Inc.

For information about special discounts for bulk purchases, please contact Simon & Schuster Special Sales at 1-866-506-1949 or business@simonandschuster.com.

The Simon & Schuster Speakers Bureau can bring authors to your live event. For more information or to book an event contact the Simon & Schuster Speakers Bureau at 1-866-248-3049 or visit our website at www.simonspeakers.com.

Designed by Jacquelynne Hudson
Motion Picture Art and Photography ©2011 Anchor Bay Entertainment, LLC. All Rights Reserved.

Manufactured in the United States of America

10 9 8 7 6 5 4 3 2 1

ISBN 978-1-4391-7174-5
ISBN 978-1-4391-7175-2 (ebook)

Dedicated to Betty, Ray, Sue, Ray Jr.,
Lee, Christian, and Camille

ACKNOWLEDGMENTS

I would like to thank the following individuals and organizations for their contributions to this project:

Jim Ahearn; the Akron, Ohio, Police Department; the Bakersfield, California, Coroner's Office; Michael Bartone; Thomas Michael Basie; Lisa Beck; Tom Bird; Kimberly Bonvissuto; Tom Buford; the California Crime Commission; the California Office of the Attorney General; Lou Capasso; Bob Cermak; Sister Veronica Cipar; *Cleveland Magazine*; the Cleveland Heights, Ohio, Police Department; the Cleveland Police Museum; Cleveland State University (Cleveland Press Archives);

Judge Donna Congeni-Fitzsimmons; Faith Corrigan; Vince Crawford; the Cuyahoga County Common Pleas Court; Susan Daniels; Sandy Deak; Carl Delau; Peter DiGravio; Bob Dinsfriend; Peter Elliott, U.S. Marshals Service; Sister Barbara Eppich; the Euclid, Ohio, Police Department; the Euclid Public Library; the Federal Bureau of Investigation; Jim Fiore; Judge Norman A. Fuerst; Gary Garisek; Rich Gazarich; Lloyd Gladson; John Griffith; Ron Guenttzler; Dennis Gunsch; Heather Hall; Richard T. Henshaw; Scott Hodes; John Carroll University; Emily Johnson; Wayne Kapantas; David Kerr; Lora Kong; Sue Kovach; Vic Kovacic; Dr. John Langer; Jim Litnar (Licavoli); Mike LoPresti; Mike Malone; Carmen Marino; Jim McCann; Nan McCarthy; Patricia Meade; Ann Millett; the Moreland Hills, Ohio, Police Department; the National Military Personnel Records Center; Dennis Nicklas; Lisa Nussbaum; J. Kevin O'Brien; Doris O'Donnell-Beufait; the Ohio Organized Crime Investigative Commission; Mike O'Mara; Bill Ouseley; Tony Paglia; Pat Parisi; the Parmadale Catholic Home; Paul Patterson; Dick Peery; the Pennsylvania Crime Commission; the Pennsylvania State Police,

Bureau of Criminal Investigation; Lennie Piazza; Joe Plisevich; Rocco Poluttro; Skip Ponikvar; Lee Porrello; Ray Porrello; Dan Poynter; George Qua; Michael V. Renda; S. A. Reuscher; the late Bill Roemer; Tom and Marilyn Ross; Bob Rowe; St. Jerome's Catholic High School; Gini Graham Scott; Susan Porrello Shimooka; Bernard Smith; Roger Smyth; Don Stevens; Chuck Strickler; James Ridgway de Szigethy; Barbara L. Tajgiszer; Bruce Thomas; Judge William K. Thomas; Serell Ulrich; the United States Federal District Court; the United States Drug Enforcement Administration; the United States Marshals Service, Witness Protection Division; Ray Villani; Joe Wagner; the Warrensville Heights, Ohio, Police Department; Joe Wegas; Adam Wezey; Sandy Whelchel; Edward P. Whelen; Chuck Whitten; Bob Wilson; Dean Winslow; Mairy Jayn Woge; Ken Wuchte; Tom Yovich; and those persons who wished not to be named.

Special thanks to the Cleveland, Ohio, Police Department; the Lyndhurst, Ohio, Police Department; Frank DeMaio; Ed Kovacic; Patrick Dearden, who encouraged me to pursue this project; Peter Miller, my book and film manager; Abby Zidle of Pocket Books; and my Heavenly

Father for His multitude of gifts, especially those of faith and perseverance.

Rick Porrello
October 2009

CONTENTS

KILL THE IRISHMAN

INTRODUCTION

FOR decades, Americans have had a fascination with the Mafia. We have paid generously to be entertained by films like *The Godfather*, *Goodfellas*, *Casino*, and *Donnie Brasco*. Likewise, millions have been spent in bookstores on titles like *Boss of Bosses*, *Double Cross*, *The Last Mafioso*, *Underboss*, and the numerous John Gotti stories. Most recently, HBO has brought us *The Sopranos*.

It started in the fifties, when mob soldier Joseph Valachi broke the blood oath of *omertà*, which swears Mafia members to secrecy. Higher ranking mob turncoats like Jimmy "the Weasel" Fratianno, Angelo "Big Ange" Lonardo, and

Sammy "the Bull" Gravano would soon follow. The term "Mafia" became a household word.

In years to come we would learn of the Mafia's influence in labor unions, gambling, political corruption, narcotics, major airports, big-city docks, and even the entertainment mecca of Las Vegas. There would be shocking allegations and hard-to-ignore evidence that the Mafia had collaborated with the Central Intelligence Agency in "Operation Mongoose," the plot to assassinate Cuban Communist leader Fidel Castro. Many even believed that the Mafia helped engineer the rise of John F. Kennedy to president of the United States, then arranged his assassination as well as those of Senator Robert Kennedy and actress Marilyn Monroe.

In the seventies and eighties, the government began winning more of its battles with the Mafia. New antiracketeering legislation and technology, coupled with tougher drug laws, undercover operations, unprecedented interagency cooperation, and WITSEC, the federal witness protection program, were effective weapons against the mob. Attrition of old-school Mafiosi made the timing right: the young replacements were not the jail-hardened men that their fathers, uncles, and neighborhood heroes were. As a result, whole Mafia hierarchies were dismantled in cities like Milwaukee, Cleveland, Kansas City, and Los Angeles. Top New York mob dons like Tony Salerno and John Gotti were convicted and imprisoned for life.

If you traced the fall of the Italian-American Mafia to one point in time and one place, it would be 1977 in Cleveland, Ohio. Numerous trials were sparked by a war of bombings for control of the underworld. In the end, those cases produced unprecedented defections, resulting in an increasing flow of intelligence and multiagency investigations that culminated in historic convictions from Los Angeles to Kansas City and from Cleveland to New York City. The origin of the whole thing can be traced to one man, an outsider, in pursuit of power and fortune—an unlikely hero who came to be known as the Irishman.

ONE

ON May 12, 1975, Lieutenant Ed Kovacic, a supervisor with the Cleveland Police Scientific Investigation Unit, was enjoying breakfast when he heard an explosion in the distance.

"Danny Greene was just killed," Kovacic said to his wife.[1]

At Greene's Collinwood district apartment, a bomb was thrown through a kitchen window. Danny was in bed with his girlfriend, Debbie Smith, when he awakened to the sound of the window shattering. He was on his feet immediately and grabbed a .38 revolver, one of several weapons he kept at the ready. He started heading for the bedroom door when the bomb exploded, blowing out one side of the building and demolishing the kitchen. A portion of the bedroom floor caved in, sending Danny tumbling down to the kitchen into a pile of rubble.

Danny's two dogs escaped from the rubble, but two of his four cats did not fare as well. They were asleep in the kitchen and awakened to the sound of the bomb being thrown through the window. Dashing over to investigate the strange object, the animals were killed instantly when it exploded.

Danny rose quickly, having suffered only a broken rib and numerous cuts and bruises. He headed for Debbie up in the bedroom. She had also narrowly escaped death as an air conditioner was blown in from the window, landing inches from her head. Leading his stunned girlfriend by the hand, Danny confidently picked his way through the rubble. They made it safely outside to Greene's Lincoln and left the area before Kovacic and other police arrived on the scene. Bomb squad investigators found a second device at the rear of the demolished building. The package consisted of a large chunk of C-4 plastic explosive strapped to a five-gallon can of gasoline. Experts later discovered that the blasting caps were faulty. Witnesses reported hearing what sounded like two gunshots moments after the two bombs exploded. Those were the blasting caps, but they were not large enough to detonate the C-4. If the second bomb had gone off, half of the block would have gone up in flames. It did not, lucky for Collinwood. And lucky for Danny Greene.

Police were at no loss for potential motives in the bombing. It could have been the strong-arm tactics Danny used in his labor consulting firm. It could have been his alleged involvement as an enforcer in the firechaser racket. (Firechasers monitored radio fire calls to be first to offer building owners board-up and repair services.) Or perhaps it had something to do with another violent act in Cleveland's underworld only two weeks earlier: the murder of notorious racketeer Shondor Birns. Whatever the motive, Ed Kovacic had no doubt about the intent.

"There are three reasons someone bombs someone," he told a *Cleveland Plain Dealer* reporter. "Either it's to make someone start doing something, make someone stop doing something, or to kill someone. This was to wipe out Danny Greene."[2]

By this time in his life, Danny had given many

dangerous men the motive to wipe him out. Un-
daunted, he would continue his quest for power
and eventually cross paths with members of the
Mafia, a powerful crime organization that ruled by
murder. Danny's appearance on their radar screen
would start a bomb of his own ticking—one that
would wreak havoc on ruthless men who were
suddenly incapable of stopping one man whose
passion was his own courage and audacity.

Several days later after the bombing, the rubble
was cleared away, leaving an empty lot. Danny had
two trailers brought in, one for his residence and
the other for an office. He had a sign erected outside his trailers announcing: "Future Home of the
Celtic Club." A green harp, a traditional Celtic
symbol, adorned the sign. And overhead, fluttering
in the breezes off Lake Erie, was the Irish tricolor.

Near the street, Danny would sit bare-chested
on a lawn chair or wooden bench, making himself an easy target for his enemies but waving to
his admirers. Some of them were needy neighbors
and recipients of Greene's generosity, such as a
free turkey during the holiday season. Not since
the Prohibition days of Chicago's florist racketeer,
Dion O'Banion, had there been such a powerful
and colorful Irish-American gangster.

TWO

O N November 9, 1933, John Henry Greene and his girlfriend, Irene Cecilia Fallon, appeared before a justice of the peace and were legally married. They were both twenty years old and had been brought from Ireland to America as children.

Five days later Irene Greene was checked into Cleveland's St. Ann's Hospital, where all Catholic women of her time gave birth. Devastated for months by the shame and embarrassment of Irene being pregnant out of wedlock, the two families were offered temporary joy in the birth of her and John's healthy baby boy.

But something went terribly wrong. Joy turned

to fear. Though the delivery had gone well, the young mother began hemorrhaging. As her condition continued to worsen, Irene Greene was moved to the intensive care ward. Several days later she died. Doctors listed her cause of death as an enlarged heart.

It was a tragedy that continued to take a toll on the families for years to come. The baby's identity remained simply "Baby Greene" until Irene's funeral and burial. Afterward, John Greene decided to name his son Daniel, after the baby's paternal grandfather.

Shortly after the death of his wife, Greene began drinking heavily. He lost his job as a Fuller Brush salesman and moved in with his father, a newspaper printer, himself recently widowed. Unable and unwilling to provide for his son, Greene placed the child in an orphanage.

About ten minutes by car south of the Cleveland city limits is the large suburb of Parma. It was here, in 1925, on 180 acres bounded by a farm, that the world's first Catholic cottage-plan village for boys was built. A life-size statue of Jesus embracing several children still welcomes visitors. Parmadale was designed to provide homes for the rapidly growing orphan population but took in, to a larger extent, neglected and dependent children, especially those whose parents could not afford to care for them at home. Instead, they paid a small fee for their children to be housed and educated by the nuns of Parmadale. Most of the parents, many struggling immigrants, made regular visits when their busy work schedules allowed.

The mission at Parmadale was to provide the children with a haven from fate's cruelties and turn their lives around, returning them to society with a better chance at happy and productive lives. Two nuns lived with the boys in each of the cottages and tried to duplicate normal life. It was not unusual for boys to be raised to maturity at Parmadale, which was hailed as a model of public welfare. In the case of Danny Greene, however, Parmadale was not a success.

At the time of young Danny's birth, the nation was still reeling from the Great Depression.

In the years following "Black Thursday," October 24, 1929, dozens of banks would fail, the unemployment rate would soar to an all-time high, the homeless would flock to soup kitchens, and farmers would be evicted from their land.

During Danny's childhood, a sinister force

prospered, seizing the nation in a network of crime that would weave its way into the very fabric of American society. This force was part of a tradition bred centuries earlier in Sicily, the largest island in the Mediterranean. By the nineteenth century, Sicily had been conquered by so many different people that the natives came to distrust all forms of government. Instead, Sicilians depended on a secret society of honorable men who provided the poor and oppressed with protection, stability, and pride. This society, the Mafia, relied on two codes, *omertà* ("honor") and *vendetta* ("vengeance"), to keep the peace. It became an unwritten rule in Sicily to leave the government out of private affairs.

As the Mafia grew in influence, its leaders grew greedy for wealth and power and its mission became corrupted. But for the native Sicilians, the Mafia, for all its sins, meant stability and patriotism. These traditions and attitudes were brought to America at the turn of the century by the millions of immigrants hoping to escape poverty and oppression in the Land of Opportunity.

By the 1920s, most of the major cities from Chicago to New York were home to a significant underworld presence. Business owners threatened by bankruptcy turned to mob loan sharks for cash, and thus took on new partners. Powerful labor unions were coming under Mafia control, and many high-level police officials and politicians were increasingly "on the pad."

As this force matured, battles between the Mafia, other ethnic organized-crime groups, and independent gangsters were occurring in major cities across the nation. The struggles began with the 1919 passage of the Eighteenth Amendment and the Volstead Act, which forbade the sale and manufacture of ethyl alcohol. Referred to as the "noble experiment" by President Herbert Hoover, with Prohibition came the birth of nationally organized crime as various underworld groups partnered to maximize profits and reduce the bloodshed that brought heat from the law. And the Mafia would become *the* organized crime force to be reckoned with.

In most cities, conflicts were waged over control of booze, gambling, prostitution, and territories. In Cleveland, the most dramatic war was over corn sugar, the primary ingredient of then-popular corn liquor, also known as bourbon, long a money crop for generations of farmers.

Joseph "Big Joe" Lonardo was Cleveland's first

Mafia boss and figured prominently in the sugar war. Around the turn of the century, Lonardo, his three brothers, and their friends, the seven Porrello brothers, immigrated to Cleveland, Ohio. In 1911, Big Joe and his wife, Concetta, had their first son, Angelo Anthony Lonardo. His godfather was Anthony Milano, an underworld figure becoming prominent in Cleveland's Little Italy district.

The Porrello and Lonardo brothers worked together as corn sugar wholesalers and bootleggers before the Porrellos started their own operation. Both families amassed small fortunes, but their luck ended in 1927 when the Lonardos' former business manager, Salvatore "Black Sam" Todaro, engineered the murders of Joe Lonardo and his brother John, giving the Porrello family a lock on the corn sugar market. At the time, Todaro was working for the Porrellos, and his actions started a war.

Eighteen-year-old Angelo Lonardo swore revenge for his father's murder—and used his unwitting mother as bait. On a sunny afternoon in 1929, Angelo drove her down to the Porrello sugar warehouse and shouted to a Porrello employee. He said his mother wanted to talk to Sam

Todaro. Always respectful of Big Joe's widow, Todaro approached the car, unconcerned with caution. As he got close, Angelo thrust a revolver out
the window and fired six times.

Angelo Lonardo was eventually arrested by
the Cleveland Police, convicted, and sentenced
to life for killing Todaro. But victory for the CPD
was short-lived. Within eighteen months, clever
attorneys for the Lonardo family won Angelo
a second trial. But the eyewitnesses responsible
for the first conviction ignored subpoenas to return from Italy, where they had fled in fear. Angelo was subsequently discharged and released.
His courage in personally avenging his father's
murder and his success in court earned him the
respect of Little Italy's Frank Milano, to whom
the former Lonardo soldiers had pledged their
allegiance.

After Big Joe Lonardo's murder, Joe Porrello
became the Mafia chief in Cleveland. His reign
didn't last long, however. In 1930 he and his
bodyguard were shot down in a Little Italy restaurant owned by Frank Milano. Other sugar war
violence left another Lonardo and three more
Porrello brothers dead. In the underworld, the
transfer of power is usually accomplished through

murder. In this case, the Cleveland mob reins were seized by Frank Milano.

Milano had connections to powerful Italian and Jewish mobsters in New York City. As a result, he won a seat on the mob's newly formed national ruling commission. The commission comprised the heads of the five Mafia families in New York City and the bosses of the Chicago and Cleveland mobs. Situated roughly halfway between Chicago and New York, in an ideal stopover point for traveling gangsters, Cleveland's Mafia enjoyed a powerful reputation for several decades. But eventually their rule would be challenged by an Irish upstart determined to take control.

THREE

DANNY Greene was taken out of Parmadale by his father in 1940; he was seven years old. John Greene was dating a nurse. The couple married and moved into an apartment, preparing to start their own family, so Greene brought Danny home to live with them. But the new Mrs. Greene ultimately rejected the boy. Danny ran away from home several times, undoubtedly seeking the affection provided by the Parmadale nuns. Eventually John Greene gave up on uniting his son with his new family.

Danny was then taken in by his grandfather. They lived in the upper unit of a two-family wooden shingle house on East 147th Street, a short block of modest homes in the east side Cleveland neighborhood known as Collinwood. For the rest of his childhood years, Danny lived with his grandfather and, for a time, an aunt also. John Greene apparently abandoned his son; when Daniel's father died in 1959, the newspaper's death notice listed only the children he had with his second wife. Daniel was not acknowledged.

While living in Collinwood with his grandfather, Danny Greene attended school at St. Jerome's Catholic School on Lakeshore Boulevard. There was no tuition for most parochial schools then, only a nominal book fee, so even struggling families could provide their children with a Catholic education. Though bright, Daniel lacked motivation and fit in poorly with the formal and disciplined structure of Catholic school. Separation of the sexes was strictly enforced at St. Jerome and most other parochial schools of the time: boys on one side of the class, girls on the other. It was the same routine at lunch, recess, and Mass. And at the end of the day, the students again divided in two groups: those who lived east of the school and those who lived west.

Most of the kids at St. Jerome developed a

great fondness for the nuns and priests. Even Danny developed lasting friendships with some of his teachers. Several of the nuns were sympathetic to Danny's situation, and tried to help where they could.

Sister Barbara Eppich, a fellow St. Jerome student, recalls, "Because his grandfather worked nights and slept days, Danny would often come to school hungry, tired, and dirty. Some of the nuns would take him down to the school kitchen, get him something to eat, and clean him up. And if he was overly tired or didn't have his homework done, his teacher would have him move his desk to the hallway, where he could finish his assignment or even sleep. Because Danny was such a good baseball player, his teachers wanted him to be rested for his games."[1]

For a time, Danny even served as an altar boy. But more often he preferred dice games with his buddies and fights on the streets instead of school books. Often while the boys were shooting dice the police would pull up, confiscate their change, and send the boys on their way. Sometimes the cops herded the boys into the back of the cruiser and drove them around the block, letting them off where they had picked them up. The boys would be found in the same spot shooting dice again in a couple of days.

Danny was a good friend to have. Even at a young age, he was loyal and always willing to lend some change to a buddy—or join in a brawl. He was athletic, excelling at baseball, basketball, and boxing. Even though he was a poor student who often got into trouble, the nuns of St. Jerome let him play sports because he was too valuable to the school teams.

Danny was a handsome lad of average build, with blond curly hair and darting, alert blue eyes. Though he had little adult guidance and did not often submit willingly to authority, Danny did have respect for his elders, perhaps a result of his years in Parmadale. Combined with his natural charm, he was well liked by the neighborhood adults. Many sympathized with the motherless boy, abandoned by his father to be raised by a grandfather who was seldom around. Danny's paper route was a lengthy task, due to the mothers who would stop him to chat, and maybe offer a bag of cookies to take home, before the boy could continue on his way.

Danny was especially liked by the McDuffy family. Sean McDuffy was in Danny's class at

St. Jerome. But it was Billy McDuffy, eight years Danny's senior and already driving, whom Danny most admired. He loved to run errands for Billy, who was generous in compensating Danny with whatever change he had in his pocket. Mrs. McDuffy also took a liking to the "mischievous young lad," as she called him.

Once, Mrs. McDuffy gave Danny a dollar bill to fetch a loaf of bread from the local baker. Danny was quick about the errand, returning within ten minutes. But he earned Mrs. McDuffy's wrath by bringing her two stolen loaves of bread and the same dollar bill. Mrs. McDuffy refused to accept the bread and sent Danny back to pay for one and return the other.

Danny had a knack for finding trouble—and getting out of it. One of his regular partners in mischief was Joey Wagner, a good friend who often stayed with him. Danny and Joey joined the Boy Scouts together, but it was soon clear that they were far from model scouts. Skipping the first two meetings, the boys went to a local pool hall to shoot a few games. The next week they were finally forced to attend a meeting, since their parents had been informed that the boys would be bringing home important paperwork. It was their first and last meeting. They arrived late and took seats near the edge of the curtain at one end of the rough semicircle of scouts on the dusty stage. The scoutmaster walked back and forth in front of the curtain, addressing his troop. His voice echoed through the small gymnasium, pausing occasionally as he reviewed the honored traditions of the Boy Scouts of America. Most of the proud new scouts listened intently, but such boredom was not the evening Danny had planned.

As the scoutmaster turned away, Danny whispered something to Joey, then quickly slipped behind the curtain. Joey's eyes widened in anticipation and fear as he glanced back and forth from the scoutmaster's face to Danny's hand poking out from underneath the curtain. Danny waited for the scoutmaster to stand still, then ever so gently managed to stick a wooden match between the sole and the upper of the scoutmaster's shoe. Danny lit the opposite end of the match with a lighter, then quickly slipped back around the curtain to take his seat. A few seconds later, whoosh!—a "hot foot"—as the tip ignited in a tiny blue and orange burst of sulfur, starting the scoutmaster into a jig and the troop into a roar of laughter. It was a practical joke right out of a

Three Stooges comedy and attempted only by the most daring boys.

The scoutmaster shouted for order while he extinguished his shoe and checked for damage. Then he conducted a very brief investigation. It wasn't difficult, since several of the boys, still snickering among themselves, were pointing at Danny Greene. To further incriminate themselves, Danny and Joey could not stop laughing.

The scoutmaster escorted Danny and Joey out of the school, promising to inform their parents. Danny wasn't worried.

FOUR

DANNY got his first taste of the more informal and permissive life of public school when he started ninth grade at Collinwood High. He was picked up quickly by the basketball team and proved to be an excellent team player. But lack of interest in his studies was still a problem— and so were a handful of Italian ruffians. Off the basketball court Danny was a loner, a seemingly easy target for bullying, the cocky Italians figured. But they figured wrong. Danny feared nobody and would stand up to several boys at once, proving his talent and experience with his fists. But this lack of fear, this refusal to knuckle under, perpetuated bad blood between Danny and several of the numerous Collinwood Italians in the years to come.

Danny's grandfather figured that public school was a mistake and signed Danny up the next year at St. Ignatius High School on the west side of town. Joey Wagner also attended St. Ignatius, so he and Danny used to hitchhike to school together. Danny found St. Ignatius to be a long trek. He overslept too many days and his grandfather could offer little help after working nights at the *Cleveland Plain Dealer*. He came home too late in the morning to get the boy off to school. The routine didn't last long and Danny was expelled. From there he went back to Collinwood High School. But Danny had plans for a more adventurous lifestyle, one that did not include school books or homework. In 1951, he dropped out of high school and headed for a U.S. Marine Corps recruitment office. A few weeks later he was inducted and shipped off to boot camp.

While Danny was serving in the Marines, young men in Little Italy and Collinwood were idolizing veteran wise guys. The mysterious lifestyles, fancy cars, and clothing of mobsters like Frank Brancato, John Scalish, and Angelo Lonardo were magnets for many misguided boys.

Among those young men who fell in with the gangsters were John Nardi and Jimmy Fratianno, two local Italian boys who'd already had their own brushes with the law. Employed by a vending machine workers' union to sell the services of their repair technicians, Nardi threatened a dissident bar owner and was arrested. Eventually the charges were dropped, but his methods caught the attention of Ohio Teamsters leader and jukebox baron Bill Presser and Tony Milano, a Cleveland Mafia leader.

By the late forties, Presser had taken on Nardi as a partner in several jukebox companies. During that time, Nardi was also running a Little Italy booking operation—and dating a niece of Milano's. Not long after Nardi married into the family, Tony Milano got him into Teamsters Vending Machine Service Employees Local 410, founded by Bill Presser. Eventually, Nardi was elected secretary-treasurer, but he had other ambitions and sought an ally in Danny Greene. The goals of both men would put them on a collision course with James "Jack White" Licavoli and his cousin, Leo Lips Moceri.

Licavoli and his cousins, Peter and Thomas "Yonnie" Licavoli, were bootleggers in St. Louis.

In 1926, James was shot in the leg and arrested after a wild chase and shootout with Saint Louis police. But the Licavolis had influence on the streets and in the courtrooms: though he had fired on officers, James was charged only with carrying a concealed weapon—and even that charge was dropped. Later James followed his cousins to Detroit, where they had wrested control of the city's rackets from the original Purple Gang. There a bootleg conviction bought him a stint at Leavenworth. When he was released, he joined his cousins in Toledo, Ohio, where they had moved to avoid the heat from the murder of a crusading anti-Mafia radio broadcaster.

The Licavolis were not in Ohio long. Yonnie and four others of his gang were arrested for the murder of a Toledo beer baron. Pete Licavoli returned to Detroit and regrouped, taking the name of the Purple Gang for themselves. James Licavoli eventually settled in Cleveland and was "made," or officially inducted, into the Cleveland family. He became wealthy from vending machines and gambling enterprises, especially the infamous Jungle Inn near Youngstown, Ohio. Originally a brothel, the Jungle Inn was an open casino offering huge crowds of gamblers craps, a Greek dice game called barbut, chuck-a-luck, roulette, cards, and even bingo for the ladies. During its operation numerous murders and disappearances were traced to the casino and its associates.

Licavoli and his cousin Leo Moceri became close friends with Jimmy Fratianno. Moceri, nicknamed "Lips" because of his thick lips, spent time in California, where Fratianno became a made member of the Los Angeles Mafia. The mobsters proved themselves as cold-blooded murderers and often reminisced about their hits while playing pinochle. In the years to follow, Moceri returned to Ohio. Fratianno stayed in California but remained close friends with Moceri and Licavoli, who eventually inherited leadership of the Cleveland mob. By that time, two unlikely outsiders wanted control. And they would kill to get it.

FIVE

DANNY served most of his time with the Marines in the Fleet Marine Force Division at Camp Lejeune. He gained respect in the boxing ring, taught firearms, and was promoted to corporal in 1953. After being honorably discharged that year, he moved to New York City, where he met June Tears. The couple fell in love, married, and moved to Cleveland, where Danny took a job as a brakeman in the Collinwood rail yards.

The marriage didn't last long and brought no children. In 1954, Danny left his wife and filed for divorce, alleging "gross neglect of duty and extreme cruelty" by June Thomas Tears Greene. The court granted the divorce, alleging that June had a husband living at the time she married Danny. How devastating—a bigamous bride! But Danny recovered quickly.

In 1955 he met an attractive brunette named Nancy. He told her nothing of his marriage to June Tears, and before his divorce was granted in 1956, the two married. They had two daughters.

By this time Danny's uncle, an attorney, suggested that he could make a better living on the docks. So, in 1957, Danny left the railroad and became a member of Local 1317 of the International Longshoremen's Association, or I.L.A.

The sixties were the glory years for the Port of Cleveland. In 1959, the opening of the St. Lawrence Seaway added 8,300 miles of seacoast to the United States and Canada. With access to the Atlantic Ocean, immensely profitable overseas trade was suddenly made possible for 95,000 square miles of freshwater lakes in the states of Ohio, Minnesota, Wisconsin, Michigan, Illinois, Indiana, Pennsylvania, and New York and the Canadian provinces of Ontario and Quebec.

Cleveland spent $10 million to ready the waterfront for the arrival of overseas shipping. At its peak, the northern Ohio port city averaged nine thousand ships per year through the harbor, dropping off twenty-one million tons of iron ore, automobiles, grain, and general merchandise. They were impressive numbers for a relatively small port that was ice-locked four months out of the year.

Longshoring is a small but furious world of winches, crates, pallets, lifts, cranes, and diesel smoke. If a ship ports during the night, longshoremen may have to work in foggy, damp weather. Often workers are transients with questionable backgrounds, but there is a strong camaraderie among these often foulmouthed, tough-talking, bluest of blue-collar workers.

Longshoremen work in gangs and are employed by the stevedore company that owns the cranes and other heavy equipment used to unload ships. The greenhorns drop into the holds of a ship to strap and chain giant containers of cargo. Cowhides are worst for the men in the hold because maggots and salt fall on them as the loads are being raised. Signalmen give heavy crane operators the okay to raise the load up. The favored workers might get a gravy assignment like checking. They merely wait for the pallets to be extracted from the ship and then inventory the load with a tally sheet. Other dockworkers use lift trucks to warehouse the cargo.

While becoming established as a longshoreman, or "dockwalloper," as they have been dubbed on the Great Lakes, Danny busied himself reading in his spare time. He was especially fond of books about Celtic and Irish history, particularly the legends of the fearless Celtic warriors. It was a part of his troubled past that he could be proud of. Danny liked to share his knowledge of Celtic history with his fellow longshoremen, most of whom were Irish.

The Celts were one of the great barbarian peoples of Europe during the five hundred years before the birth of Christ. They were known for their ferocious and skilled warriors and were a people almost constantly at war. They were unusually clean for their era and were well built, being so conscious of their physiques that obesity-prone warriors were fined. They were an impetuous people with extravagant pride. Some tribes undressed completely before going into battle, the better to show off their impressive builds and heavy gold jewelry while taunting their enemies. The Celtic warriors cultivated two arts with great success: the art of clever speech and the art of war.

The Celts believed that after death they joined the very gods they worshipped. For them, death was the center of a long life, not the end. Celtic warriors were not afraid of death. They would consider it an insult to their honor to run from a collapsing building. Certainly this lack of fear fed their courage. Above all else, the Celtic warrior wanted to be remembered as a hero whose exploits would live on in history.

Danny's ethnic pride was contagious and, combined with his charismatic personality, he attracted friends easily. Within only a few years of joining the dock union, Danny Greene had become one of its more popular members.

In the meantime, Danny's tangled romantic history continued. In 1960 Nancy filed for divorce, accusing Danny of gross neglect of duty. They divorced that year. Several months later, Danny wanted to get remarried. Not daring to deny him, Nancy agreed. In 1961 he began a relationship with another woman, eventually fathering two sons and another daughter with her.

By now Danny was reading books like Leon Uris' *Trinity*, a true-to-life novel about Irish oppression by the British. And even as he was enjoying Budd Schulberg's *On the Waterfront*, the classic tale of corruption on the docks of New York City, he was witnessing questionable practices by Walter Weaver, Local 1317's president. Weaver was operating as an employer in contracts for the unloading of grain ships. Unions were created to unite workers for the improvement of their working conditions and fringe benefits, so for Weaver to control hiring was an obvious conflict of interest. But it allowed him more control over his membership. Danny recognized the benefits that Weaver enjoyed—the doling out of assignments, control of union finances, an office, and prestige in the labor union community—and he had a vision for himself. If a position of leadership in the union came available, then Danny Greene would pursue it with ferocity. In the meantime, his reputation would grow.

Unloading ships is tough, hectic, and dangerous work, second only to mining in work-related injuries and deaths. A prayer was even composed in the early sixties after two longshoremen were killed in work-related accidents. The "Stevedore's Prayer" was believed to be the first prayer written specifically for longshoremen. It received the approval of the Catholic Church and was introduced at a special open-air Mass on the waterfront. The prayer read as follows:

> *Lord Your name is holy, help us to remember it.*
> *You worked beside the lake like we do;*
> *Your eye is our signalman;*
> *Your pallet of grace holds every load;*
> *Your strength lightens every lift;*
> *These works are our daily bread.*
> *Forgive us when overtime in work or sin makes*
>   *us undermine You.*
> *Help us to forgive our enemies.*
> *Our labor is Your labor.*
> *Every day we handle Your cargo.*
> *Watch over us, Lord, body and soul,*
> *You know how much we need You.*
> *One of these days we will come Your way.*
> *Amen.*

But not every injury or death was an accident, especially in the early days of the Cleveland port.

When stevedore official Sigvald Refsnes caught Danny Greene sleeping on duty in the hold of a ship, he fired him. A few days later, a heavy piece of machinery fell on Refsnes, seriously injuring his leg. Refsnes spent several months recuperating but eventually had to have his leg amputated. Danny's involvement was never proven, but one thing was for sure: he was on his way to becoming a force to be reckoned with.

SIX

IN 1961, Walter Weaver, president of Local 1317 of the International Longshoremen's Association, came under fire by the international union for operating as an employer. When Weaver was removed from office, the international president met with the union officers in search of someone to run things until an election could be arranged to choose a new local president. Someone independent of the current administration would be needed. There were several choices, but the international president was most impressed with Greene's charisma, popularity, and speaking skills. As a result, he appointed Danny as trustee to run the local in the interim. Danny campaigned for the local presidency, and when the special election was held, he won the vote handily. In a separate election, he was also voted in as district vice president of the Great Lakes office of the I.L.A.

On his lapel, Danny wore a custom-designed diamond-studded I.L.A. pin. His hair had darkened a bit since his days as a blond child and was more wavy than curly. He had a ruggedly handsome face with some pockmarks and full lips. His naturally high forehead was accentuated by hair loss, which he eventually minimized with painful transplants. He took pride in his new position, seeing himself as part of a growing tradition of Irish-controlled U.S. ports.

To start, Danny ordered the dilapidated I.L.A. headquarters cleaned up and kept that way. Even the bathroom sparkled, and seldom could a piece of litter be found in the union hall parking lot. Like the Celtic warriors before him, Greene took his personal hygiene very seriously. He even had a nail brush in the union bathroom to keep his well-manicured nails scrubbed clean.

Danny had a section of the union building remodeled into a spacious office for himself. It was outfitted with plush green carpeting and rich mahogany furniture. A meeting room was furnished with a huge mahogany table. In later months, Danny would begin hosting parties at the I.L.A. hall before and after Cleveland Browns games, with prominent judges and councilmen among the guests.

Greene would say that before he took over, the I.L.A. headquarters was a closet with a packing crate and a lightbulb on a cord. His renovation of the union hall included a fresh coat of paint. The color? Green. Danny even had the union bylaws reprinted in green ink and used green paper to post announcements on the union bulletin board. The color green was an obsession that became Danny's trademark.

Paintings of former presidents Harry S. Truman and Franklin D. Roosevelt hung on his office walls. In his bookshelf were *The Last Hurrah*, about the life of James Michael Curley, former Boston mayor, and *The Enemy Within*, by former U.S. attorney general Robert Kennedy. Near his desk were bronzed busts of President John F. Kennedy and Jacqueline Kennedy. Proudly displayed between them was a mint Kennedy half-dollar in a presentation case.

He purchased baseball-style I.L.A. jackets

(green with white leather sleeves) for a handful of tough officers and loyalists, men like brothers Chauncey and John Baker and Leon "Skip" Ponikvar. Danny dubbed these men his "inner circle." Essentially they were his enforcers. Using intimidation and bullying, they kept the members, even foremen and supervisors, in line.

Most of Greene's initial changes drew little more than chatter from the I.L.A. members, but some caused quite a stir. For instance, he ordered the lobby window closed and locked, thus eliminating the formerly open view of the inside offices. Instead he had a single phone placed in the lobby. Members and visitors would have to pick up the phone and explain their presence in this forbidding place to someone on the other side. Then—maybe—they would be seen by one of Danny's officers or, under rare circumstances, by Danny himself. For members coming in simply to pay dues, they just had to drop their money in a dues slot newly built into the locked office door.

During his first and one of his very few meetings with the membership, Danny raised the annual dues by about 25 percent. He also fired more than fifty members, claiming they were winos and drifters. Some of the members complained about the changes, which distanced them from their labor representatives and made a fortress out of their union hall. But their complaints fell on deaf ears. Danny seemed to have a mysterious perception about who was saying what, who was complaining, and who might be provoking others. Rumors swirled that some of them were spying for Greene. Anyone who complained or slandered Danny risked a beating from members of his inner circle, also known as the "grievance committee."

Danny's rise to labor union leader brought many enticing benefits to a man who had never experienced power, recognition, or wealth. He used all of his considerable charisma to ensure his time in the spotlight. To foster relationships with officials of other labor unions, Danny insisted on his men working their picket lines, especially where there was television coverage.

"Those are my men out there," he'd boast.[1]

To cement his authority, Danny needed a system to control the men who might get in his way. He found that control in the hiring hall, in effect making the I.L.A. an employer like his predecessor, Walter Weaver, had done. The Local 1317 hiring hall was a shanty next to the union headquarters where the men who wanted to work that day would gather in the morning in what is called a "shape-up," a casual method of employment selection that had been abolished at some ports. To get work, men called a special phone line at union headquarters. A tape recording, updated daily, gave the dock number, the number of gangs needed, and the starting times. Those who wanted to work that day would meet for the shape-up, each with the hope of being chosen to receive a work ticket entitling him to a day's wages.

Danny announced that the hiring hall was a place where Irish kids could get a decent day's pay. In reality it was a significant part of Greene's calculated plan to obtain dictatorial power on the docks. With the hiring hall in place, he could now dole out choice assignments to loyal members, and the dirtiest and most dangerous to those who challenged his control. And he'd have leverage to use against the shipping companies.

Danny had I.L.A. linemen, the men who tie the ship up when it docks, work the incoming vessels. But when one shipping company insisted on using its own anchor men, Danny just sent in the least experienced and slowest I.L.A.

linemen. Some of the rank-and-file members also adopted this hostile attitude toward the stevedore companies. Often things got ugly, with Greene's men shooting out lights in warehouses or smashing windows on cranes. On one occasion gunplay caused a German freighter to depart before being unloaded. When the shipping companies threatened to start docking sixty miles to the east, in Ashtabula, Ohio, Danny shut down the Cleveland port and brought the situation to a head.

Losing thousands of dollars each day, the stevedore president, who is employed by the shipping companies to unload their cargo, was forced to sit down with the brazen Danny Greene. With no leverage to negotiate (some say because Greene got him drunk), the stevedore chief signed a collective bargaining agreement giving the I.L.A.— that is to say, Greene—the exclusive privilege of employing workers on the docks. The shipping companies would announce how many gangs they needed, and Danny, through his Best Labor Service, would choose the men. He would be paid an average of $4,000 per ship by the local stevedore company. And just like that, Danny Greene, labor "peacemaker," stopped all the strife that was costing the stevedores and shipping companies thousands.

As a new union official with access to large amounts of money—membership dues, special work fees, and payments from the shipping companies—Danny could socialize with men who had achieved the success he hungered for. One of his west side favorites was the Blue Fox Restaurant and Lounge. There, Danny could often be found with Adrian "Junior" Short. Since 1965, Short had been president of local 27 of the International Alliance of Theatrical Stage Employees. He ruled the stagehands' local like a personal fiefdom and was said to keep a .22 in his jacket and a sawed-off shotgun in his desk drawer.

Soon Danny had a newly purchased pistol in his own desk drawer. And, like the Celtic warriors who constantly honed their battle skills, Greene practiced target shooting in the union hall at night. To provide security for the hall and to run errands, Danny hired ex-boxer and railroad buddy Arthur Snepeger, who was also an explosives expert.

Short Vincent Avenue, named for its diminutive length, was the festive hub of Cleveland's downtown entertainment district in the sixties.

Angelo "Big Ange" Lonardo, scion of the Mafia family who battled the Porrello brothers during Prohibition, operated the Tastee Barbecue and later the Frolics Bar there. A rising star in Cleveland's Scalish crime family, Lonardo later became a partner in Captain Frank's seafood restaurant on the East Ninth Street pier.

In the middle of Short Vincent was the venerable Theatrical Bar and Grill, where bookies and B-girls rubbed elbows with well-to-do tourists, suburbanites, attorneys, and judges. For decades, it was the social headquarters for many Clevelanders, including organized-crime figures. Featuring fine food and top entertainers on its elevated stage, the Theatrical was a favorite stop for visiting celebrities such as Eddy Duchin, Frank Sinatra, Lauren Bacall, and Jimmy Durante.

It was at the Theatrical that Danny Greene took a liking to a waitress and brought her to the docks to work as a union secretary. He provided her with a new car, raffling off the old union-owned vehicle to the members—a seemingly generous move. But in fact all the members were issued raffle tickets, even those not interested in the car. A letter from Greene accompanied the tickets. It read in part: *You have been issued five (5)*

books of tickets for which you are responsible, regard-
less of whether you sell them or lose them. The face
value of the tickets is $30.00.[2]

While making his nightly rounds, Danny met
several men who would figure prominently in
his life. Louis "Babe" Triscaro was a mobbed-up
Teamsters Union boss who had a day laborer service. Danny set up a side business with him. When
extra hands were needed on the docks, Greene
hired them from Triscaro. To maintain eligibility
to work, the employee had to pay a work fee. Triscaro then kicked back a percentage of the fee to
Danny. It was another way for Greene to line his
pockets at the expense of his union members.

John Nardi, business partner of Teamsters
boss Bill Presser, was secretary-treasurer of Teamsters Vending Machine Service Employees Local
410. Nardi had interest in becoming an inducted
member of the Cleveland Mafia, and as a nephew
of Cleveland mob consigliere Tony Milano, he
seemed to have the right connections.

Alex "Shondor" Birns, a notorious Jewish
racketeer enjoying his golden years, was still active in the numbers racket, enforcing peace among
the mostly black operators. Danny would eventually do muscle work for Birns and Frank "Uncle

Frank" Brancato, who had been a longshoreman himself in his younger days and maintained ties with the dockworkers' union in New York City. Brancato was allied with John Demarco, head of the Licatese faction (men with roots in Licata, Sicily) of the Cleveland Mafia and aligned with the better-known Scalish regime.

Demarco and Scalish were laying low after their arrests at the 1957 raid on the national Mafia gathering in Apalachin, New York. There, dozens of top mobsters from across the country had attended a failed crime convention. The media attention given to organized crime as a result of the Apalachin meeting subsided but picked up again in 1963 when Joseph Valachi, a soldier in New York's Genovese crime family, agreed to cooperate with the federal government. It was the first time an insider had betrayed the mob's code of silence, a betrayal punishable by death. Valachi's testimony publicly confirmed the presence of a nationwide crime syndicate.

John Scalish became wary of the serious damage that defectors could cause and took precautions against the risk of turncoats like Valachi. As a result, he brought little new blood into the Cleveland mob as the membership aged. Scalish's failure to maintain the organization would have dire effects on its ability to face challenges from outsiders in coming years.

Danny Greene would learn much from these aging mobsters. And he'd come away believing that there was no reason why the Irish, instead of the Italians, could not sit at the top of the crime food chain.

SEVEN

BY 1964, Danny Greene, labor union president, was living the good life.

"He'd bring four or five of us to the Theatrical and pick up the check," recalled Skip Ponikvar, former longshoreman and Greene loyalist. "He had portraits taken of the officers and put in nice frames. He'd attend district conferences in Detroit or Milwaukee and bring his officers. He bought himself a green Cadillac. All of it was paid for by the local."[1]

But the initiation fees and monthly membership dues weren't enough to fund Danny's lavish spending. So in 1964 he negotiated a contract with Sherwin-Williams and International Milling to pay the I.L.A. a lump sum for the unloading of their grain and flax, used to make paints, flour, and cereal. The union then issued paychecks to the longshoremen.

From these grain loads, Danny pressed for "voluntary" paycheck deductions to go toward a newly established building fund to be used for re-modeling the union hall. Some of the longshore-men were told they could donate $25 in cash to the fund, but most opted to volunteer their time unloading the grain boats.

Grain is among the most dreaded loads for longshoremen. The work is dusty, hot, and dan-gerous. Fortunately, about two-thirds of the grain is unloaded via an enclosed conveyor that is sent into the hold, pulling the product out and trans-ferring it directly into the storage building. But then the crews must take over, donning protec-tive masks to prevent their lungs from filling with dust. They descend into the grain hold and wade in up to fifteen feet of grain or flaxseed, then guide mechanical plows to scoop the leftover grain onto the conveyor.

Longshoremen unloading grain worked only one half hour in these nasty conditions. They emerged from the hold soaked with sweat and covered with dust. In the winter, they ran to a buddy's car to keep warm for their half-hour break. At the end of payday, the men endorsed their checks and turned them over to union officials. But it didn't stop there. For many, what was supposed to be six or ten hours of donated time turned into one hundred, two hundred, even three hundred hours of free work. Those who complained or refused to work the grain boats were all but forced into retirement. For most, this was not an option: they knew no other way to make a living. If they were picked for any work during the morning shape-up, it was for the filthiest, toughest jobs. Skilled machine operators could even wind up in the ship's hold, unloading maggot-infested cowhides, if they did not cooperate with Greene's plans.

It was about this time that Danny received a phone call from Marty McCann, an F.B.I. agent investigating a longshoreman who had left a gun in his Detroit hotel room after attending an I.L.A. convention. McCann made an appointment to speak with Danny about the incident but in reality had other ideas. McCann was the head of a newly established organized-crime squad and was well known for his ability to develop informants.

Though courageous and determined, McCann was also personable and approachable—some of Greene's own traits. And, of course, McCann was of Irish descent.

The men hit it off and soon Danny was accepting invitations by McCann to meet in secret on a regular basis. But Greene's only concern was how he might work the relationship to his advantage. And he could do so by providing McCann with tidbits of information he gathered from the many organized-crime contacts with whom he associated with.

McCann wasn't the only lawman Greene developed a relationship with. Ed Kovacic was a good-natured but street-toughened Cleveland police supervisor. He had a problem with several longshoremen who were getting drunk and terrorizing a neighborhood in his district and went to the I.L.A. headquarters to speak with Greene. Danny arrived chauffeured by two longshoremen. One of the dockworkers opened the car door and Danny stepped out wearing a men's white fur coat belted at the waist.

"I think we're about to meet Marlon Brando," Kovacic whispered to his partner.[2] It was the start of a love-hate relationship.

Though Kovacic hungered to put Danny in prison, the two men maintained a decent personal relationship. They would talk about Danny's children, sports, and the Collinwood neighborhood. Ed even coached Danny's son in football. But sometimes their talks grew heated.

"If I tried to approach him with anything he was involved in, it almost always came down to who would throw the first punch," Kovacic recalls. "He would push you as far as you would go. He admired people who had guts, people who stood up to him. If you bent, he had no use for you."[3]

As Danny became increasingly generous with union funds generated by the grain boat scam, some longshoremen left the docks to pursue different employment. A few of the most persistent members were kept in line, tough-talked, or strong-armed by the few union bosses and timekeepers in the gang who did get paid. It was shakedown city at the Cleveland International Longshoremen's Association, and Danny Greene was making money—and a reputation.

But longshoremen are a tough lot. They began complaining to vice president Chauncey Baker. Originally one of Greene's inner circle, Baker had become a popular and influential officer who had recruited many of the dockworkers. The complaints turned into heated allegations, so Baker approached Greene about stopping the grain ship volunteering. The operation was putting too much money in Danny's pocket at the expense of the workers. By that time Danny had moved Nancy and their two daughters to a stately home in the Cleveland suburb of Willoughby. For protection, he bought a German shepherd. Danny's greed had clouded his judgment, and he rejected the well-meant advice.

"No, we continue. And you know what, Chauncey? Maybe we should part. I'm putting you back on the docks."

Seeing Baker as a threat to his control, Greene assigned Chauncey to a small area of the dock, hoping to reduce his influence among the longshoremen. Then he called in Chauncey's brother, John, an I.L.A. business agent.

"Where do you stand in this argument, John?"

"Blood's thicker than water, Danny. I'm with my brother."[4]

Danny promptly removed John Baker from the offices and put him alongside Chauncey on the docks.

The beginning of the end for Greene's I.L.A. career came when stevedore manager Sigvald Refsnes returned to the docks a year after losing his leg in the suspicious accident. Refsnes was a Norwegian merchant fleet captain who had settled in Cleveland. He had married *Plain Dealer* journalist Faith Corrigan.

When Refsnes heard of Greene's building fund shakedown operation and arrangements with Best Labor Service, he was furious. He informed his wife, who fired off a letter to the *Plain Dealer*'s managing editor:

> *I have been informed by a reliable source of a situation on the docks here in Cleveland which warrants investigation. A company called Best Labor Service, Inc. with offices at 3030 Woodland Ave. . . . supplies longshoremen to the stevedoring companies. The men are hired daily since the requirements for their services vary according to the work— 20 one day, 50 the next. They are paid by the stevedoring [firms] the regular longshoreman's rate, which I believe is close to $3 an hour. However, the checks are delivered to an agent of Best Labor, which is entitled to cash them.*

*The workers get $1.25 an hour of which 17
cents is charged as a fee. The rest goes to
Best Labor. The workers are mostly Negroes,
many illiterate and falling under the heading of
"moving meat." They have no idea how much
money they are really entitled to and that the
papers they sign give Best Labor the right to
this exorbitant fee. Cleveland Stevedore has
a contract with the union to get all their labor
through the union and the rumor on the docks
is that Danny Greene, the I.L.A. head here
is behind Best Labor Service since the workers
are union members. On the books, Greene
gets $6,000 a year salary from the union
but he drives a new Cadillac automobile and
displays other material forms of wealth . . . I
hear the Cleveland Stevedore Co. is beginning
to supply the men with their check stubs so
that they will know just how much they made.
This needs confirmation. The hourly scale for
longshoremen is $2.68 an hour. By contract
with the I.L.A., laborers must be hired
through the union, which means calling Danny
Greene each evening. Men from the Best
Labor outfit show up for the jobs while the
union hall . . . has men sitting around waiting*

*for jobs. The only way the Best Labor outfit
could learn about the jobs is through Danny
Greene . . . You will be supplied with a list of
the laborers involved in the next week.*

                                    Faith[5]

Faith Corrigan's editor assigned an aggressive
reporter named Sam Marshall to investigate. Six
weeks of anonymous phone calls, secret meetings,
and undercover work were capped with signed affidavits from a score of fed-up but nervous longshoremen.

"Why was it necessary to work for nothing on
the grain boats?" Marshall inquired of several of
the men. From each, he received the same answer:

"Well, if I didn't work grain boats for nothing I wouldn't have been hired the next day or
it would have caused some sort of friction on the
job," one replied.

"If I wanted to work, I had to work the grain
boats or I wouldn't be hired for any other work,"
said another.

Greene was quick to defend himself, blaming
his problems on dissident union members.

"The members have volunteered to donate
all their grain boat checks if they want to offset

the deficit created by our building program," he told Marshall. "If they wanted their money they could have it. You've been talking to a few dissidents. We have the program posted on the bulletin board."

He also denied that members had to work for free on the grain boat to be eligible for regular paying work.

"Most certainly not. We've spent money to set up a system to ensure that all available work is equally distributed. Those are all dissident members," Greene insisted.

Marshall conducted hundreds of interviews and spoke with shipping company officials.

"I've been aware of what's going on but I couldn't get anyone's ear, and I couldn't prove it," one stevedore boss complained. "No one ever had these problems in the fifty years of relations before Danny Greene took over. He's intimidated them to the point where nobody would say anything, but apparently the *Plain Dealer* has broken through. Someone ought to go to jail for this. They're exploiting the common working man and now these poor guys are having trouble making a living."

U.S. attorneys had heard enough and obtained

a court order requiring Greene to surrender all of the I.L.A.'s financial records. Court officers tried to serve the subpoena but Danny could not be located. The next day, in a surprise move, Danny called a special membership meeting. The dockworkers responded with a record turnout. Greene made a brief appearance, maintaining his innocence even with these men, the victims of his greed. He went so far as to place blame on the membership for failing to bring forward their dissatisfaction and even denied knowing of the grain boat practice.

"If you don't want the grain boat operation by the union, speak up," Danny told them.

Immediately after the meeting, Greene was served with the subpoena for the court records. Later, in an interview with Sam Marshall, Danny defended the surprise meeting as "routine" and denied seeking a vote of confidence.

"Sure I rule with an iron hand, but that hand is with society and the port, not against them," he maintained.[6]

But reporter Sam Marshall was as unrelenting as a terrier after a rat. Despite the cautions of Ted Princiotto and other *Plain Dealer* managers, he pressed on with the exposé. The coverage won the praise of union members, city officials, and stevedore officials.

By then, a large number of I.L.A. members filed the following petition with the national union:

> We, the undersigned members of Local
> 1317, do hereby petition the president
> and executive board of the International
> Longshoremen's Association to place our
> local in trusteeship immediately, so we can
> hold a free election for leadership of our
> choice. Further we ask the international
> president and his executive board to send
> a representative from the international
> office to our local's membership for the
> purpose of discussing in detail each one
> of the points outlined in the attached
> report. Finally we ask the international
> president and his executive board to act
> at once as we, the undersigned, are fearful
> of other unions' attempts to take over
> this work which is our livelihood and so
> much of which has already been lost to
> neighboring, non-I.L.A. ports through
> our leadership's unlawfully called strikes,

slowdowns and through a reign of fear and treason to their own union brothers.[7]

Following the petition, the longshoremen staged a work stoppage. Skip Ponikvar was there in the morning when the men refused to show up. He made a frantic call to Danny.

"They ain't shaping up, Danny. I think we lost control."[8]

"Don't worry about it," Danny said.

WEARING A CONFIDENT SMILE AND A CONSERVATIVE brown suit adorned with his diamond-studded I.L.A. lapel pin, and carrying several small manila files, Danny Greene greeted Sam Marshall at Federal District Court. He continued to maintain that his problems were the result of "a few dissident I.L.A. members."

"The records are all there, Sam," he said, shaking hands with the lone newspaperman who had brought him so much trouble.

Danny had grown skilled in the use of publicity. His charming personality and natural talent for rhetoric were an effective combination. Danny was quite cunning in this regard, but it wasn't just street smarts. As a child, he had shunned textbooks but instead sought to learn from books about great leaders, politics, and history. And it was obvious that he emulated the brave warriors of his ancestry, both in his eagerness for a fight and his silver tongue.

But Sam Marshall knew better. Greene's assurance that "the records are all there" sounded convincing in the newspapers, but Danny hadn't even provided a fraction of the files that were subpoenaed.

Joining U.S. attorneys in the investigation of Greene were the U.S. Department of Labor, the Federal Bureau of Investigation, the National Labor Relations Board, and the Internal Revenue Service. Also aiding the effort was the Organized Crime and Racketeering Section of the U.S. Justice Department, still enjoying national recognition for their success in the investigation of the International Brotherhood of Teamsters. As a result of that probe, national president James Hoffa and over 150 union officials were convicted of racketeering.

The dock investigators made numerous findings in the days that followed. The case against Greene took off after they searched his office, a procedure that uncovered substantial financial records Danny had refused to produce. Evidence showed that Danny had failed to pay any contributions to the welfare system. After weeks of review by special auditors, it was revealed that Greene had a very simple though illegal method of operating his union's finances.

"We have found no records of any separate funds in the financial records we have gone through," a U.S. attorney reported. "Greene apparently operated everything from one fund."

Investigators made another startling discovery in Greene's office: part of Danny's original refurbishing of the union hall included an elaborate system of tiny hidden microphones. The bugs were secreted in strategic locations and wired into phone lines to give Danny full coverage of conversations in the lobby, the meeting room, and the parking lot. Even the bathroom was bugged. The control panel, which had recording capabilities, was located in Danny's office, concealed behind a secret sliding panel. A stack of ten twelve-inch tapes sat nearby.

Sam Marshall was on hand for a demonstration of the eavesdropping system by local interim officer Chauncey Baker.

"You're on this tape, Sam," Baker informed Marshall. "In a telephone conversation."

Danny had more problems. The day after the eavesdropping equipment was discovered, someone fired several bullets into his home. Though it was 11:00 p.m., Danny was supposedly downtown meeting with his attorney. His wife, Nancy, and their two young daughters were home alone.

A reporter interviewed a frightened Nancy Greene about the incident:

"I went back downstairs to watch television," Nancy recalled. "At first I thought it was just something happening outside. Danny has gotten other threats, but nothing like this has ever happened before. I was so upset last night, I couldn't even write down for the police what happened."

Only Danny's German shepherd heard the shots and the glass breaking. The dog's barking prompted Mrs. Greene to investigate and call the police, who found the bullet holes.

"How is Danny doing?" the reporter asked.

"His Irish is up and he's fighting for his job," she said.

"What happens if he doesn't get it back?"

"He might lead a normal life then."[9]

The next day, the same reporter telephoned Danny to interview him about the shooting.

By now Greene was feeling the heat of the

dock investigation, and the shooting of his house didn't help matters.

"Why don't you ask that crusading newspaper of yours that prints only one slant of a story?" Danny growled. "I'm sick of the racket. Consult my lawyers for any comment."

Danny hung up on the reporter but later prepared the following statement announcing his resignation from Local 1317 of the International Longshoremen's Association. It was a typical display of Greene's rhetorical skill:

> Effective immediately, I have resigned as an officer and member of Local 1317, International Longshoremen's Association and as vice president of the Great Lakes District, International Longshoremen's Association. I have dropped any affiliation with the Longshoremen's Association and any connection with the labor movement. After nearly four years of devoting all my energies to get the dock workers in Cleveland a fair shake, I now find that my only compensation is headlines in the newspaper and bullets through my windows. Before March, 1961, I was a

longshoreman working in the holds of ships when I was asked to take over this union and make something of it. Under my administration the union has moved from a tiny office in a dingy building to fine quarters near the waterfront where members could be proud to gather. The pay envelopes of Cleveland dock workers have increased 40% and $200,000 in welfare funds have been accumulated to care for the future and security of the men. Winos and drifters have disappeared from the waterfront. Criminals and pilferers have been dismissed. Decent men supporting families have taken their place. Experienced men now have job protection instead of depending upon the whim of a foreman for employment.[10]

In the end, the multiagency investigation produced enough evidence to indict Greene for embezzling roughly $35,000 from the I.L.A. and for falsifying union records. In 1966, he was convicted of three counts of embezzlement and two counts of falsifying records. He was sentenced to five years in prison but the sentence was suspended, apparently because it was his first offense. Greene appealed, and in 1968 the conviction was overturned by the U.S. Sixth Circuit Court of Appeals on a technicality. In 1970, the case was disposed of when prosecutors agreed to drop felony embezzlement charges. In exchange, Danny pled guilty to two misdemeanor charges of falsifying union records. He was given a hefty fine and barred from working in any labor union business for five years.

Being a confidential informant for the F.B.I. had its benefits.

"He was fined $10,000 but only paid $2,000 and was never imprisoned," recalled *Plain Dealer* reporter Mairy Jayn Woge. "And nobody knew why."[11]

FOLLOWING HIS RESIGNATION FROM THE I.L.A., Danny Greene started Emerald Industrial Relations with the backing of Frank Brancato. For a hefty price, the labor consulting firm offered "protection" against union discord, supply problems, and work stoppages. Of course, most of the problems were manufactured by Greene. For instance, Greene was able to get a load of glass held up at a New York dock. Only when the construction firm came up with a $2,000 "consultation fee" did the glass find its way to Cleveland. Most companies paid up rather than suffer expensive delays.

If someone gave Danny a problem, he'd pay Art Snepeger to blow up a business or car as a warning. If the blast generated news coverage, Snepeger got a bonus. Danny also had Art bomb a bar owned by one of the union officials who had opposed him during his days as a dockworker. Danny was not one to let a score go unsettled.

After a Dallas-based building firm complained about a ghost employee scam on its construction site, an investigation was begun by Cleveland Police. The case took them to Dallas and St. Louis and back to Cleveland, where Danny Greene's extortionist tactics had brought downtown construction almost to a halt. Investigators returned with numerous cardboard boxes of evidence. It looked like Danny Greene was again headed for some serious trouble with the law.

Affidavits were presented to a federal judge charging Greene with labor racketeering and violation of his parole, which prohibited him from working in the labor movement for another two years. It looked like an open-and-shut case until the judge, suddenly and without explanation, announced that he was dismissing the allegations.

It was a full year before investigators learned that their efforts to convict Greene had been stymied by J. Edgar Hoover. The organized crime intelligence being supplied by Danny Greene was so valuable that he warranted the protection of the F.B.I. director.

EIGHT

BY the sixties, the hauling and disposal of rubbish was becoming an attractive business. As private and public industry continued to grow, so did the tons of waste they produced. Efficient and relatively clean Dumpsters, roll-off containers, and off-site options were replacing overflowing, fifty-five-gallon drums and back rooms filled with cardboard boxes of putrid garbage awaiting pickup. Before this, rubbish haulers often carried sticks to fend off hungry rats. Though the nature of solid waste disposal was not appealing to the average businessman, the future for rubbish hauling looked promising. As business increased, small waste-hauling firms opened. Their owners were typically tough, street-educated entrepreneurs with ambition. There was bound to be conflict. And since there was money to be made, the Mafia was bound to be part of it.

Two rubbish haulers had already founded the Cleveland Solid Waste Trade Guild with the idea of eliminating undercutting and price fixing and guaranteeing a fair piece of the waste disposal profits for members. Like his fellow mobsters had done in New York City, Brancato wanted to take over control of the local $25-millon-a-year rubbish hauling industry. By infiltrating the Cleveland Solid Waste Trade Guild, he would have access to membership dues and route fees. Brancato had just the man for the job: Danny Greene, now done with the legal battles that followed his resignation from Local 1317 five years earlier. Danny muscled into the Cleveland Solid Waste Trade Guild and appointed Art Snepeger as an officer. He assigned Snepeger the task of soliciting new members. Danny also brought on board Mike Frato, a rubbish hauling friend he was so close with that they named sons after each other.

Known as "Big Mike," Frato was a barrel-chested, three-hundred-pound soft-spoken man with an engaging personality. He loved children, fathering fourteen with three different wives, and hoped someday to open a home for neglected boys. Frato got his start in rubbish hauling in 1957 with $700 and one truck. In the following years, he was able to expand to eighteen trucks with a gross income of $1 million a year. He was a hard-working, successful businessman who also had a percentage of a local service station, but a nagging gambling habit kept him in debt.

As Danny took to his assignment with zeal, the owners and employees of outside companies became victims of intimidation and violence. In December of 1969, a bomb exploded at the rear of a rubbish hauler route salesman's home. In March 1970, a fire destroyed the office and three trucks of another company. Other rubbish haulers reported threats, assaults, and even being shot at.

In the summer of 1970, Frato left the guild. "He didn't like what was happening to people who refused to join," said his wife, Susan.[1]

"The guild was a beautiful thing at first," Mike Frato told a *Cleveland Press* reporter. "But the wrong people took control. I didn't need it anymore. You might say I was expelled."

"Who got control of the guild?" the reporter asked.

"I don't want to talk about it."[2]

Mike Frato started his own organization: the Cuyahoga County Refuse Haulers Association. He had only a few members, but it was a slap in the face to Greene and his Mafia backer, Frank Brancato.

ON OCTOBER 31, 1971, A SQUAD OF CLEVELAND Heights detectives watched as young ghosts and goblins completed their joyous tour of the city's side streets. With shotguns at the ready, the officers concealed themselves in the vicinity of City Hall. The detectives chatted and joked in their two-man unmarked cars as they continuously scanned the area for anything or anyone suspicious. Earlier in the day, an anonymous caller had informed a police dispatcher that someone was going to blow up City Hall.

A half mile down Mayfield Road from City Hall, toward Little Italy, the busy street is crossed by Coventry Road. Coventry Village, a popular entertainment district, was a sixties hangout for hippies and bikers and home to a jumble of head shops, unique-gift boutiques, ethnic restaurants, and saloons. On the northwest corner of the intersection sat Swan's Service Station, in which

Mike Frato was a partner. Next to Swans' was a three-story brick building that housed the office of Frato's Cuyahoga County Refuse Haulers Association. Frato parked his Cadillac at Swan's Service Station when he visited his office.

At 12:30 a.m. it happened: an explosion rocked the intersection of Mayfield and Coventry. Detectives from the City Hall detail were on the scene in seconds. Calls flooded the police switchboard as fire equipment was dispatched to Swan's.

The service station was heavily damaged from the blast, and windows in nearby buildings were blown out. Inside, detectives found a smoldering, badly damaged Cadillac. A few feet away they made a gruesome discovery. It was the body of a man lying facedown against a nearby wall. Judging from the vicious loss of his arms, face, and chest, he had been at the center of the powerful blast.

The detectives ran a computer check on the license plate of the Cadillac and found that it was listed to Michael Frato. But the dead body was not his. Frato had been playing cards in an office across the street when his car was bombed. The police cordoned off the area and began investigating. The Bureau of Alcohol, Tobacco and Firearms, the Cleveland Police Intelligence Unit, and the coroner's office were called in to assist.

ART SNEPEGER HAD BEEN AN ALL-PURPOSE errand man, loyal to Danny Greene since their days on the railroads and docks. He had experience with dynamite, occasionally working with cement contractors to blow out tree stumps. He had handled some bombings for Greene, but when Danny asked Art to commit murder, he misjudged his friend.

In September, Snepeger fixed a bomb on Frato's car but had second thoughts. He had grown up with Frato in the Woodland Avenue "bloody corner" neighborhood and was deeply involved, but Danny was going too far. Snepeger removed the bomb from Frato's car, telephoned Big Mike, and informed him of Greene's plan.

Several days later, Snepeger received a phone call from then-sergeant Kovacic of the Cleveland Police Intelligence Unit. Kovacic was working on the bombing of a grocery store and wanted to question Snepeger. He knew Snepeger was involved, but he had no evidence—so he bluffed, threatening to charge him with arson. The bluff worked infinitely better than Kovacic had predicted. Snepeger produced a forty-page statement regarding the criminal activities of Danny Greene and several other Cleveland gangsters. Most interesting to Kovacic was Snepeger's revelation that Greene was indeed an F.B.I. informant. Kovacic had suspected as much for several years.

A few weeks after Snepeger talked to Kovacic, Danny contacted Art, demanding that he return to work for him. On the evening of October 31, Snepeger was on his way out of the house when he spoke briefly with his girlfriend about the situation.

"I've gotta go back to work for Danny cause I'm dead if I don't. And I'm dead if I do," he said.[3]

It was the last time the girlfriend ever saw Art alive. Shortly after the Cleveland Heights bombing, police identified the disfigured body from Swan's Service Station as that of Snepeger. The police and Bureau of Alcohol, Tobacco and Firearms agents located his car near the bombing scene. Inside they found a remote control for an electric dog-training collar and various bomb parts.

The police knew that Snepeger died while

planting a bomb on Frato's car by order of Danny Greene. But why the bomb went off prematurely, they couldn't say for sure. Some investigators felt certain that the explosion was an accident caused by a radio signal, possibly from a shortwave radio or a passing police car. Snepeger's girlfriend was convinced that Art's death was a murder arranged by Danny Greene.

Though the case was never officially solved, Sergeant Kovacic received information that Greene had waited at Snepeger's car while Art planted the bomb. When Snepeger returned to the car, Greene told him that he wanted additional dynamite affixed to the bomb. When Snepeger went back to Frato's car, Greene pressed the button on the detonator.

Figuring Greene would abandon his plans if there was a heavy police presence in the area, Snepeger likely made or arranged the anonymous call. Using City Hall as the intended target would have guaranteed an aggressive response by police. And giving an inexact location would put lots of cops in the area, but not so close that Danny would figure Art had tipped them off. It was a desperate plan for Snepeger, who felt his dilemma was hopeless. Unfortunately for him,

City Hall wasn't quite close enough to Swan's Service Station for police surveillance to be noticed by Greene.

But fortunately for Mike Frato, he now had a clear warning that his life was in danger. He bought a gun. A close friend, Gus Palladino, accompanied him everywhere and sometimes spent the night at his house. It was a tense time.

"On one occasion, Mike came home late," his wife, Susan, recalls. "He ran in the house, grabbed his gun, and told me someone had followed him home. He motioned toward several cars parked in the high school lot across the street. We were up all night watching out the window. Suddenly, at 5:30, a car pulled into the driveway and stopped near the street. Mike ran out, shoved the gun in the driver's face, and yelled, 'I've got you now. Who are you?' It turned out to be our tenant's brother, who had arrived to help his brother with his paper route. We talked about the threats and he told me, 'Well, even if I am killed, I've done everything I wanted to do.'"[4]

TWO PATROLMEN HAD JUST FINISHED INTERVIEWING the victim of an assault at St. Luke's Hospital emergency room. They were pulling out of their parking spot when a Buick Riviera was driven urgently into the lot.

"There's something wrong with the passenger," one of the officers said.[5]

They stopped, got out, and approached the driver, who was just getting out. The officers observed that the passenger was slumped over and asked the driver what happened.

"I don't know," he replied before walking into the emergency room.

The officers checked the passenger, a large man who was slumped against the door. Though dead or unconscious, the man's girth had kept him in a seated position with his head halfway out the open window. Closer inspection by the officers revealed a bullet wound to the man's head and pools of blood on the seat and floor. Inside the emergency room, the driver told a nurse, "There's someone bleeding out in the car."

"What is your name?" she asked.

"What in the hell do you need my name for if there's someone bleeding in a car?"

The male walked away and moments later the police officers walked in and asked the nurse where he had gone. She motioned in his direction and the officers hurried after him. As they got closer, he ran off. After a short chase through the hospital, they took him into custody. His name: Gus Palladino.

In the meantime, doctors went out to the car and checked the passenger, who was dead. When homicide detectives arrived on the scene they identified him as Mike Frato. Later that afternoon, detectives received an anonymous phone call stating that Frato had been out gunning for Danny Greene.

The investigation of Frato's death turned toward Greene, who seemed to be mysteriously absent. Detectives checked all of his usual haunts, to no avail. Two days went by, then Danny telephoned Cleveland Police detective Jim Fuerst, whom he had known a long time. He told Fuerst he was at a motel in Painesville, Ohio, and wanted to turn himself in to straighten the matter out. Fuerst and his partner made the forty-five-minute trip to Painesville.

"Danny was waiting for us when we arrived," Fuerst explained. "He said, 'I'll tell you the truth, Jim, exactly what happened.'"

"I was walking my dogs," Greene stated. "I finished and was walking to my car when I saw this car approaching. This passenger leaned out from the front seat and hollered, 'I got you now, you son of a bitch.' He fired three shots from a pistol from only about fifteen feet. I pulled out my revolver and fired just one shot. I didn't even know I hit him. The car drove off at a high speed."[6]

Whether Frato shot at Greene to kill him or merely scare him was never determined. Later it was learned that Frato was armed and had a previous opportunity to kill Greene.

"I was within twenty feet of him," Frato confided to a friend. "I thought about doing it but I couldn't."[7]

Ultimately, the self-defense claim worked and the case against Danny was thrown out before it went to trial.

NINE

WHILE Danny Greene continued his quest for fame, fortune, and power in the underworld, Shondor Birns was considering retirement. Though twenty-six years older then Greene, Birns shared a similar childhood.

In November of 1920, Shondor was thirteen when his mother was tending to the ten-gallon still in their apartment. A faulty gas connection caused an explosion. Scalding mash spewed out and flames engulfed the young mother's clothing. Screaming, she ran outside, where a passing motorist helped extinguish the flames and drove the young woman to the hospital. Horribly burned over 75 percent of her body, she died the next morning.

Like Danny Greene at Parmadale, Shondor was sheltered for a time in a Jewish orphanage, where he made many friends. He grew up quickly, taking on a job as a newspaper boy and fighting for busy street corners during the newspaper circulation wars. Like Danny, Shondor excelled at athletics, especially baseball and swimming. On the streets he developed a reputation among the neighborhood kids as a fighter, proving himself worthy in innumerable tangles with street thugs. He learned quickly to apply the Old Testament justice of "an eye for an eye."

Shondor was drafted by mob leader Maxie Diamond, who was associated with Bill Presser. For a time, the newspapers called Diamond "Cleveland's Number One Racketeer."

Birns became a ranking member of Diamond's gang during the battles for control of the city's dry cleaners and launderers. Then the real tangles with the law began: a stolen car conviction and an assault rap in which Birns broke the jaw of a motorist who had taken too long to make his turn in front of Shondor.

With eighteen arrests in a twelve-year period, Shondor was on his way to notoriety in northeast Ohio. He basked in his fame, enjoying the attention in an almost endearing, pathetic manner. But he developed a knack for beating the charges. In that same time period, he was successfully prosecuted only twice.

During the late thirties, Shondor Birns became heavily involved in protecting whorehouses, or "vice resorts," as they were dubbed by the newspapers. He operated freely and with the blessing of local Mafiosi. Many of Shondor's clients were judges, politicians, and ranking police officers. They would be important contacts for Birns in the future, as he would be for them.

During the forties, Shondor became involved with local Mafiosi like Angelo Lonardo. Together they took control of the black-run numbers racket and profited well for many years, investing in restaurants and nightclubs.

While Lonardo was quiet and reserved, Birns was loud and operated much more openly. He enjoyed his notoriety and therefore found it necessary to invest in relationships with corrupt police officials. By the seventies, however, Shondor had mellowed, playing handball daily and spending several hours on lunch and a cocktail or two at the Theatrical, where he always sat at the end of the bar. Businessmen and attorneys, even judges, paused from their lunches and busy conversations to wave and call out, "Hi, Shon."

Birns once told a reporter, "If I'm the city's biggest crook, why do they all want to be my friend? I'll tell you why. Most of them are worse than I am, and they know that I know."[1]

Birns had recently been released from a prison stint for bribery and didn't want any more trouble.

"Kid, I don't break any provisions of parole," he once told his young parole officer. "I'll tell you why. If I go back to jail, I'll die there."[2]

After lunch, Birns would head to the Silver Quill or Christie's Cabaret and socialize while he nursed another cocktail. He talked of retirement to Florida but still had easy money coming in from the numbers racket. He had been serving as a peacemaker among the operators, settling disputes that would otherwise end in stabbings and shootings. He also laid off or distributed big bets to other cities like Pittsburgh, so no single operator lost too much if a number came up.

But the civil rights movement had come and blacks were gaining a sense of independence. Some of the operators balked at answering to a white man. What Birns needed was muscle. Gutsy Danny Greene would be just the man. Shondor had known him since Danny's days as waterfront boss.

During one of Danny's first assignments, he was supposed to toss a bomb at a dissident numbers man who was holding out on Shondor's fee. Danny parked a block down the street and pulled the igniter. But he was unfamiliar with the military-type detonator and the fuse was burning faster than he had anticipated. Danny fumbled with the bomb and tried to throw it out the passenger window, but it hit the door frame and bounced back in the car. Greene opened the door to escape. He just barely made it out of the car when the bomb exploded, blowing the roof off the car. Greene got up and walked away.

Danny would later claim that Irish luck saved his life. His worst injury was to his right eardrum: the blast left him hard-of-hearing for life.

His story to the police was that somebody had driven by and thrown a bomb in his car.

It was about this time that Danny decided to open a cheat spot—an after-hours drinking and gambling club—on the east side. He pitched the idea to Birns, who agreed to loan Greene $70,000. Most of the investment money came from members of New York's Gambino family who were friends of Birns. Problems developed when Birns insisted that Greene hire a certain man to handle some of the business at the club. The man turned out to be a drug dealer and decided to use some of the $70,000 to finance a drug deal on the side. Police were already investigating the man, and a raid on his apartment resulted in his disposing of the cocaine by emptying it out a fourth-story window. To make matters worse, the club itself was raided only a day before it was to open.

Relations between the former Public Enemy Number One and ex-longshoreman quickly turned sour. They blamed each other for the loss of the money and things began heating up. Shondor demanded that Greene pay back the loan so the Gambino mobsters could be repaid.

"Fuck 'em," Danny told Birns. "Tell 'em it was a gift."[3]

Shondor was already dealing with heavy opposition from a few black gangsters who wanted the old white guy out of their racket. Times were changing. Black racketeers had long been under the thumb of the more powerful and politically connected Mafiosi and their associates, like Shondor. Now they were demanding their independence. Several close calls had made that clear.

As if Shondor didn't have enough problems to contend with, now a cocky young punk was going to take him for seventy Gs. Birns bought a Doberman pinscher to protect his home. It would have been a good time to retire.

In February, Shondor and his attractive girlfriend, fourteen years his junior, were walking downtown when a car with several black men drove by. One of them fired two shots, but neither Shondor nor his girlfriend was hit. Several months later, Birns walked into an east side bar in response to a meeting requested by several black numbers racketeers. After the downtown drive-by, Shondor must have been expecting more trouble, because he decided to bring his heavily armed bodyguard along. As Birns and his guard entered the bar, they were immediately accosted by several of the numbers men.

"We want you out of the business or you're dead!" one shouted while pulling back his coat to reveal a pistol in his waistband.

Shondor's bodyguard reacted quickly, pulling a small submachine gun from under his overcoat. Some customers scurried toward the exits. The group continued shouting at Birns as he and his bodyguard cautiously backed out of the bar and left.

To settle his dispute with Danny Greene, Birns had put up $25,000 with a bookie friend for Greene to be murdered. Several minor underworld characters, burglars by trade, took on the assignment. On the first attempt, a bomb was planted on Greene's car. But the explosive was wired improperly and it failed to detonate. Greene discovered the bomb when he pulled into a Collinwood service station for gas and the young attendant told him that something was hanging from underneath his car.

Danny disassembled the bomb himself, removed the dynamite, and brought the rest of the package to Cleveland police lieutenant Edward Kovacic. Greene gave the bomb to Kovacic and explained how he found it underneath his car.

"Danny, we can protect you. Let us handle this," Kovacic insisted. "Now, where's the dynamite?"

"It's not dynamite, Ed, it's C-4."

"Let me have it, Danny."

"I'm going to return it to the old bastard that sent it to me."[4]

THE AREA AROUND CHRISTIE'S CABARET WAS home to a settlement of Irish immigrants anchored by the celebrated St. Malachi Church.

It was a typically cold evening in March of 1975, and the old church was packed at 8:00 p.m. It was Holy Saturday, the night before the holiest of Catholic holidays: Easter Sunday. The traditional candlelight procession had just begun. It would be an ironic setting for the murder of a Jew by an Irish Catholic.

Inside Christie's Cabaret, Shondor was looking his dapper self, dressed in maroon pants, a white turtleneck shirt, and a sport coat. He sipped Hennessy with Coke and chatted with friends as go-go dancers flirted overhead. He spoke of retiring and complained about a cold he couldn't shake. Birns was happy and relaxed. He finished his drink and said goodbye to the bar owner. A regular patron and friend accompanied Shondor to the outside of the bar, where he said goodbye. Moments later Shondor reached to unlock the door of his aqua-blue Eldorado.

A St. Malachi parishioner described the explosion as a tremendously loud thump. When the shocked church members ran out to investigate, they were sickened at what they saw—and smelled.

The bomb was definitely overkill, whether intentional or not. It was C-4, a potent military explosive. Birns was blown several feet out the roof of the car and landed near the passenger door.

The man who had walked Birns to his car braved the smoke and flames to locate Shondor. Birns was still alive, though barely. His face, arms, and chest were bloodied and blackened. His head and arms convulsed violently as the man reached under Shondor's shoulders to drag him to safety. Peering through the smoke, the man quickly abandoned his rescue efforts. He had only the upper half of his friend's torso. Birns had been blown in half. His severed legs had landed fifty feet away and other parts of him were scattered across the pavement. A chain-link fence between Christie's and St. Malachi caught many of the smaller fragments of flesh and bone.

Though Birns' Cadillac was demolished, his state-of-the-art burglar alarm survived. The horn was pulsating faintly as the parking lights flickered. A dozen tattered and burnt bills—tens, twenties, and fifties—fluttered along the ground. A leather gym bag and gym shoes had been blown from the trunk. Amazingly, a paper bag of clothing from inside the car survived. It read: *Diamond's of Ohio—Fashions for Men Which Women Love*.

Police and bomb squad members worked an

entire day examining the devastated scene. Coroner's office workers spent hours collecting as many pieces of skin and bone as they could find. A total of $843 in cash was found on or near Birns' body. The Internal Revenue Service promptly claimed the money.

In the weeks to come, investigators headed down the wrong path, concentrating on several numbers operators as suspects.

"It's dumb to talk about blacks doing Shondor," one said. "Shon wasn't no bad fella. He was white but it didn't make no difference. Shon had a black soul. He was black through and through. Shit, there wasn't no racial prejudice in that goddam Shondor Birns at all. He was a helluva guy . . . No, no, they ain't going to be no more Shondors . . . !"[5]

Shondor's widow was oblivious to the conflict with Danny Greene. Birns had sheltered her from the seamy side of his life. Mourning the dearest and sweetest man she had ever known, and aware that her husband's associate was a pet lover, she gave Shondor's Doberman pinscher to Danny.

It was a year or so before Greene was blamed for killing Birns. Though Ed Kovacic heard Danny threaten Shondor, he had no direct evidence to build a case. It seemed that everyone knew who did it, but the murder remained officially unsolved. In the meantime, Danny thought his battle with Shondor Birns was over.

ON A NATIONAL SCALE, THE MID-SEVENTIES brought important changes in the country's fight against the powerful Mafia. The federal government acquired several weapons for use against organized crime, though they wouldn't be completely battle-tested until the eighties.

R.I.C.O., or the Racketeer Influenced and Corrupt Organizations Act, made it possible to penetrate the protective buffer created by the typical mob hierarchy and convict organized-crime bosses based on a pattern of criminal activity. In short, it made it a crime to be a criminal. The sweeping legislation also allowed for the forfeiture of property obtained through illegal profits. Local, state, and federal agencies were putting aside territorial disputes and organizing into highly effective strike forces. Title III of the 1968 Omnibus Crime Control and Safe Streets Act authorized the interception of oral, wire, and electronic communications by law enforcement officers investigating serious crimes. Additionally, drug laws had stiffened and WITSEC, the U.S. Marshals' witness protection program, was becoming an attractive alternative to prison time for those criminals with valuable knowledge.

The Mafia had remained protected from such espionage due to its enforcement of *omertà*. But La Cosa Nostra was going through its own changes. The secret society was aging, and the new members coming in were not the street-toughened criminals that their fathers and uncles had been. The time was ripe for inside information to do much damage to the organization. And one of the F.B.I.'s most valued informants, Danny Greene, was poised to do just that.

TEN

IN 1974, Danny Greene left his wife, Nancy, and their two daughters and rented an apartment on Waterloo Road—a fitting street name for a man at war. Making Greene feel at home was a short side street called Danny, just a block away. And East 147th Street, where he spent much of his childhood, was right around the corner. Only seconds from access to Interstate 90, Waterloo was a short commercial strip of bars, mom-and-pop businesses, ethnic food stores, gas stations, and small apartment buildings.

Danny's new home was a two-story brick building with an empty storefront, a former cigar shop, on the bottom and a large apartment on top. He rented a small house in the rear of the property and often had business meetings there. One of the first things Danny did when he moved in was spray a flourishing grapevine with weed killer because it blocked his view from a window. And inside a closet at his apartment, he kept a small arsenal: handguns, rifles, even hand grenades. Having survived several attempts on his life, Danny made caution a priority.

Danny had a fondness for telephones. He had five installed in his apartment, all of them kelly green. And in the dining room, which had mirrored walls, he set up a weight bench. In his forties now, Greene was becoming very conscious of his health and appearance. He lifted weights and jogged daily. For a while, Danny was on a diet consisting mainly of fish, seeds, and vitamins. He frequented a Collinwood fruit market and fancied Chinese food. Often, when at a restaurant, Danny ordered only a cup of hot water, supplying his own tea bag. Still, he'd leave a generous tip.

Greene became known quickly on Waterloo. Those who didn't know him were sure to find out who he was, perhaps when Danny was driving by in his green Lincoln, or when he sat on a lawn chair outside his apartment to bask in the sun.

Greene made sure the neighborhood undesirables knew who was in charge. He kicked out a bookmaker who operated out of a small Waterloo business and kept a local bar in line with personal visits. When a rowdy group of Hell's Angels thundered into town, Greene visited their headquarters with a stick of dynamite. He threatened to light it and throw it into their clubhouse until they came out to receive a warning to keep things quiet when in Collinwood.

Two doors down from Danny was an old barber named Mike whom he began patronizing. Greene became fond of the barber despite his Italian ancestry.

"I hate those fucking dagos," Danny once told the man. "You're the only one I like. If they get me with a machine gun while I'm in your barber's chair, you'll probably be going with me," Danny joked. "But seriously, if anyone ever bothers you, you make sure you come and tell me."[1]

On Waterloo Road, Danny became a favorite with neighborhood children, whom he paid five, even ten dollars for running a quick errand. The parking lot next to Greene's building was a favorite roller-skating spot. Danny used to open his window and throw out a handful of change for them to skate by and scoop up. He made frequent cash donations to needy neighbors. And if he knew ahead of time that one was stopping at the butcher shop several doors down, he would phone ahead and instruct the owner to give her whatever she needed. He'd be down later to take care of the tab.

He was a racketeer, but Danny Greene had a deep need to be liked in the "square world," as he would call it. He was a modern-day Robin Hood, but his goodwill gestures were not graciously received by all. One afternoon Danny drove to a church in a poor neighborhood to make a rather unconventional donation to a nun he had known from grade school. He knocked on the door of the convent and presented her with a bucketful of loose coins. Knowing Danny's background, the nun suspected that the coins were stolen from a vending machine and refused the donation.

Every Thanksgiving and Christmas, Danny bought fifty twenty-pound turkeys and, with the help of friends, passed them out to his neighbors. If he saw a friend or acquaintance at a restaurant, Danny often picked up the tab. The redheaded Irish-American girl who delivered Danny's newspaper could be assured of a $5 payment even though Danny's bill was less than $2.50. Eventually Danny took such a liking to the girl that he paid her way through Villa Angela Academy, a private Catholic girls' school in Collinwood. For another neighborhood girl, Danny paid for braces. And for his closest friends, Danny gave Celtic crosses that had green marble from Ireland in the center.

Waitresses loved him for his generous tips. One waitress whom Danny took a particular liking to was Debbie Smith, an eighteen-year-old Collinwood High School senior who worked at Fanny's, a very popular local restaurant. Danny brought her to work at his Waterloo Road office. There she typed and did filing, but soon they became romantically involved and Debbie moved in. Danny liked her to wear green.

By this time Danny was trying to make a name for himself in the fire cleanup and repair industry. Often referred to as firechasers, the businesses monitor fire department radio calls and speed to the scenes of burned-out buildings to propose their services to property owners. One company was emerging as supreme, using high-pressure sales tactics and threats to competitors. Bombings, fires, and other acts of violence were becoming commonplace in the Cleveland area. Greene tried to enter the scene as a peacemaker, much as Shondor Birns had with the numbers operators. For a couple thousand dollars, Danny would give a firechasing firm a guarantee against interference from competitors.

But Greene's nemesis, Ed Kovacic, and other investigators from the Cleveland Police Scientific Investigation Unit were onto him. Since Greene's days as president of the local longshoremen's union, Kovacic, who lived only one block from Danny, had been hounding him. He followed Greene around, kept abreast of his affairs, and questioned him often. Kovacic was convinced that he could learn much about organized crime from Greene. But the F.B.I. was one step ahead. By this time, Special Agent Marty McCann had cultivated Danny into a top-echelon informant. Like Teamsters boss Jackie Presser, Danny played a dangerous role, believing that the benefit of providing the F.B.I. with information about his enemies outweighed the risk of being identified as a confidential informer. He even gave himself a code name: Mr. Patrick. It was both the name he was confirmed with as a child and that of his beloved Irish saint. Danny insisted that the F.B.I. use the moniker when contacting him.

Before Danny could establish a foothold in the firechasing racket, his plans folded under the pressure of Kovacic nosing around. Greene denied any involvement in the fires and bombings.

IT WAS MAY OF 1975, AND DANNY AND HIS girlfriend, Debbie, had just survived the bombing of his Waterloo Road apartment two days earlier. The rubble had been cleared away, leaving an empty lot, and Danny Greene, the Celtic warrior, was back. Nobody was going to force him off his turf. Danny had two trailers set up in the empty lot. One would be his residence and the other would serve as headquarters for the Celtic Club.

Among Danny's top Celtic Club representatives were Kevin McTaggart, Keith Ritson, and Brian O'Donnell. Ritson was a burly twenty-eight-year-old with bushy hair. A roofer by trade, he already had arrests for burglary, carrying a concealed weapon, and possession of criminal tools.

Tall and blond, nineteen-year-old Kevin McTaggart affectionately referred to Greene as his uncle. He was a stagehand at the Cleveland Convention Center and a lighting man at the

Roxy Bar & Grille on Short Vincent Avenue. McTaggart also served as a liaison to the Hell's Angels, who were occasionally hired by Danny as muscle.

Brian O'Donnell, a bar owner and electrician, was the brightest of the crew and served as financial director. He helped Danny pass out the Celtic cross pendants, which were imported from Ireland.

Youngest in the group was Greene's own teenage son, Danny Jr., who often accompanied his dad on business errands and guarded his car. Greene's old friend Billy McDuffy frequently served in the same capacity. Other Celtic Club henchmen included an Irish-American ex–Cleveland police officer and even a black county jail official.

Greene dubbed his men with the names of famous Celtic warriors and even quizzed them on Irish history. He supplied them with green business cards and green pens to pass out. He kept in contact with them via modern belt pagers, a fairly new addition to communication technology.

After organizing the Celtic Club, Danny played the failed Waterloo Avenue bombing to the hilt, flaunting his growing legend of invincibility. For a newspaper photographer, he posed proudly in front of a boarded-up window next to his obliterated apartment building. He granted interviews to all the television stations in town and called his would-be assassins maggots. When one reporter suggested that he had nine lives, Danny said it just wasn't his time yet.

"I'm an Irish Catholic," Danny responded. "I believe that the Guy Upstairs pulls the strings, and you're not going to go until He says so. And I didn't run away from the explosion. Someone said they saw me running away. I walked away."[2]

A few weeks later, it was almost Danny's time again. He found himself a target while jogging on White City Beach. A sniper concealed several hundred feet away fired several shots at him. The man thought he would have an easy target as Danny jogged along with no cover. But instead of ducking to the ground, Danny pulled out his revolver and started shooting while running directly toward his would-be assassin, in complete disregard for his own safety. The tactic worked: the sniper fled and was never positively identified. Later it would be learned that this was an attempt to fulfill the Greene murder contract left active by Shondor Birns.

After Danny appeared on television, a young

Greene wannabe was so impressed with his hero that he honored the Irishman with a poem, "The Ballad of Danny Greene":

> Among the Crow, the story says,
> A man was judged by fiercest foe.
> Many scalps a brave Chief took,
> Who fought his way to fame,
> Often he outwitted death,
> Ere history prized his name.
> A modern warrior known as Greene
> Was very quick and smart, and mean.
> He scrambled hard and fought like hell,
> And led a charmed existence.
> They shot him down and blew him up
> With most regular persistence.
> Through guile and luck and skill,
> Danny Greene is with us still.
> He does his job as he must do,
> With zeal, finesse and pride.
> It's hard to keep a good man down,
> With Saint Patrick at his side.
> Some day he'll die, as all we must,
> Some will laugh but most will cry.
> His legend will live on for years,
> To bring his friends mixed pleasure,

For he has done both bad and good,
And lived his life full measure.[3]

Danny couldn't have been more proud.

ED KOVACIC WANTED TO PUT GREENE UNDER police protection, but Danny refused.

"They're gonna kill you, Danny, you know that, don't you?"

"Well, Ed, if they ever do get me, it's going to be with a bomb. But then again, there's not a bomb big enough to kill Danny Greene."[4]

With his confidence peaking, Danny continued to taunt his would-be executioners. Sometimes he was cautious; sometimes he was downright foolhardy. In the evening before he retired, he placed a pebble on the hood of his green Lincoln. In the morning he checked to make sure the pebble was in place, then got on his hands and knees to check under the vehicle. In the late evening hours, Greene stood in the window of his lighted bedroom, making himself an easy target. During the night, he sometimes sat in a chair on the roof of the next building, surveilling his turf for signs of intruders. At his feet was a high-powered rifle.

The police set up their own undercover detail

to protect Greene. For several weeks they guarded his property from an unmarked van. Being the vainglorious host he was, Danny once flustered the detectives by having several sandwiches and soft drinks delivered to the police van.

Across the street from Greene's trailer lived a mother of six children whose husband had recently left her. Greene admired the woman, an Irish-American named Patty, for holding her head high despite her hardships. Danny introduced himself one day and the two chatted.

"Do you know what I do?" he asked her.

"I don't care what you do. What you do is your business," she answered.

"I know you're an honest person because you look me straight in the eye. I like that you don't ask for help. You keep your problems to yourself. And I like the fact that you're Irish."

"Irish people can be cold sometimes, though," Patty offered.

"I can be cold when I want to be," Danny replied.

Knowing that Patty was facing the loss of her home, Danny offered a section of his second trailer for her and her children.

"I'd consider it a favor if you moved in. You could keep an eye on things. You know, keep it private for me."

Patty agreed and took up residence in Greene's house. Danny parked his car under Patty's kitchen window. Patty had a dog that always barked when someone walked by. But Danny didn't mind. He even encouraged her to keep the dog outside.

"You should have lived here before my building was blown up."

The two took a liking to each other and had frequent heart-to-heart chats. A bold and candid person, Patty often talked to Danny about the path he had chosen in life.

"I knew when I was fourteen I didn't want a regular job. I wanted excitement and wanted people to know who I was, to respect me. But I also wanted them to know that I have a good side despite what I do."

Patty even rebuked Greene for the danger he lived with.

"How can you go through life always having to look over your shoulder?"

"Hey, I'm Irish Catholic. I've got the best guardian angel there is," Danny replied. "Besides, the man upstairs pulls the strings. I'm not going anywhere until He says so."

"Do you think you're going to get to heaven because of all the money that you give away?" Patty asked candidly.

Danny laughed and shook his head.

"Boy, the things you come up with," he said. "That's what I like about you. Now, don't you know that all us Irish people go to heaven?"[5]

ELEVEN

I N 1975, Danny Greene attempted to establish himself in the vending machine business, which had often been a Mafia-dominated racket. Cigarette machines, candy machines, and coin-operated washers and dryers could all bring easy profits, especially if competition was limited. He partnered with John Nardi, the secretary-treasurer of Teamsters Vending Machine Service Employees Local 410 and a Mafia associate with ambition to someday take over as local mob chief. Though he harbored ill feelings toward many Italians, Greene cooperated with them whenever it was in his best interest.

Danny would find that getting into the

business wasn't so simple, especially when he met Thomas J. Sinito, a Mafia lieutenant under Angelo Lonardo. Sinito's involvement with Lonardo began when he worked as a bartender at Angelo's Highlander Restaurant and Lounge. But Sinito had several of his own ventures as well: locally, he entered the vending business with lucrative washer and dryer accounts at numerous apartment buildings. His front was a gift basket company on Chagrin Boulevard, a favored area for Mafia business and socializing.

Danny needed accounts of his own, but everything seemed locked up. When his considerable charisma didn't convince superintendents to change vending suppliers, he resorted to threats. When Sinito intervened to protect his territory, Danny planted a bomb on his car. Sinito found the explosive and destroyed it.

Other vending machine dealers competing with Greene weren't so lucky, as can be seen in this police report:

> Officers were dispatched to the Days Inn at Route 46 and Interstate 80, Austintown Township, Ohio. This officer found the body of a white male bound and gagged

with tape lying face down in a small pool of water about eight inches deep under an oak tree. The unknown male was wearing a gray tweed suit with a blue short-sleeved shirt. The unknown male's pants were pulled below his knees and all his pockets were out. The unknown male was wearing blue socks, one black 10 ½ low cut shoe, and the black right shoe 10 ½ was on the ground about 30' southwest of the body. The unknown male was wearing a gold wedding band on his left hand. The victim appeared to be 40–50 years old; 5'9" tall; weighing 180 pounds; black hair mixed with gray. The crime scene was roped off and the County Coroner was notified.[1]

The unknown male referred to in the Austintown Township Police homicide report was later identified as John Conte. Conte had had his own vending business and was a route man for another company that provided slot machines for parties and private clubs. Conte was also a friend of Joseph C. Gallo, a known mob figure, and later a partner of Sinito. Gallo had been indicted but acquitted for the earlier bombing of Danny Greene's apartment.

On the day of his murder, Conte told his wife he was going to meet with Danny Greene. Police theorized that Conte was beaten to death in Danny's trailer and the body transported to Austintown Township, in Ohio's Mahoning Valley. They conducted a search of the trailer and confiscated a baseball bat, lengths of phone wire, electrical cord, and floor tiles that had buckled from excessive moisture, possibly soapy water used to remove blood stains. The evidence was sent to a crime lab for analysis but the results were inconclusive. Danny was never officially implicated in the killing of Conte, which was reportedly ordered by John Nardi. Then another man died and opened the door wide open for Greene and Nardi to move in on the Cleveland Mafia in a bigger way. Nardi wanted to be boss. And Greene believed it was time for the Irish to have a bigger role. Their time had come.

FOR THIRTY YEARS, JOHN SCALISH HAD BEEN Cleveland's handsome, silver-haired Mafia don. A suave, quiet man, he spent much of his leisure time on the waters of Lake Erie entertaining prominent citizens on his impressive yacht. He was content to live well off the Las Vegas skim—money stolen from casino profits before being counted for taxes. Scalish also ran Buckeye Cigarette Company, known for its strong-arm tactics, with partners Frank Embrescia and Milton "Maishe" Rockman. Rockman was the mob's unofficial treasurer and link to the Teamsters union via his friendship with union president Jackie Presser.

Scalish had been plagued by heart problems and cancer for several years. In May of 1976, he went in for delicate bypass surgery. Scalish made it through the operation but succumbed several hours later in the recovery room. News of his death swept through the underworld. And the ensuing confusion about who was in charge of the Cleveland Mafia would be fortuitous for Danny Greene and John Nardi.

Although Scalish had not announced his successor, Rockman claimed that Scalish had personally informed him that he wanted Jack Licavoli to replace him. Rockman's announcement came as a surprise to many, including Licavoli, who wanted nothing to do with running the Cleveland rackets. Lonardo was considered by most to be the logical replacement for Scalish. He had more contacts with other mob families and was more familiar with Mafia business formalities.

Licavoli was an unlikely choice for Mafia chieftain. Although he had amassed a fortune from gambling enterprises, he was little more than a stingy old man, satisfied living as a bachelor in his tiny Little Italy house with the strings of garlic hanging outside the back door. Since his income had never been declared, he was even able to draw a monthly Social Security check. Lonardo didn't say anything, but he suspected Rockman of lying about Scalish's choice of successor in order to secure more influence with the new head of the Cleveland family.

Reluctantly, Licavoli assumed leadership. Up until then, the seventy-two-year-old former Detroit Purple Gang member had been content playing golf and making homemade wine. By then he was more often referred to as Jack White or "Blackie," both plays on his dark complexion.

Licavoli could often be found passing the hours on a Mayfield Road bench outside the card shop or the Roman Gardens restaurant, a short walk from his house. There the short, stout, and aging Mafioso chatted with friends and mob wannabes while he leaned on his treasured wooden cane, a prized possession that concealed a glisten-ing, razor-sharp blade.

Despite Licavoli's great wealth, he was known for being cheap and occasionally foolish to the point of embarrassment. Once at a local mall, he was detained by store detectives for switching the price tags on a pair of pants. After hearing about the background of their shoplifter, the de-partment store manager shuddered and declined to prosecute. Another time, Licavoli was caught putting slugs in a vending machine.

In Little Italy, Licavoli had control of one of the most lucrative barbut games in the region. He received a weekly profit from the fast-paced Greek dice game, which was run by Pasquale "Butchie" Cisternino. Cisternino was a tough, blue-eyed, good-looking mob associate and devoted father of four.

Licavoli named Tony Delsanter as his consig-liere and appointed his cousin Leo Moceri as un-derboss. Moceri had been running the rackets in Akron, fifty miles south of Cleveland. Leo was a muscular and active man still feared and respected nationally as a senior Cosa Nostra member. Some described him as a deadpan character with an icy stare and thick lips.

At age sixty-nine, Leo Moceri was in good health except for recent gallbladder surgery and poorly fitting dentures about which he frequently complained. He had a long history of arrests, including three murder indictments in Toledo. One was for the death of an Ohio beer baron. Moceri escaped prosecution on all three, thanks, perhaps, to his use of a whopping sixteen aliases. In 1969 he was acquitted of income tax evasion. Incredibly, he claimed that he had no income but instead was living on the profits from his days as a bootlegger. He didn't carry a gun, nor did he have one in his house. He didn't need one. Anybody who knew what was good for him would never mess with Lips.

Moceri kept quite busy loan-sharking and with various other rackets. He had numerous business interests, including real estate. He was a partner in an Akron bingo hall and received a cut of the gambling profits at the popular Little Italy Feast of the Assumption.

Licavoli's chief enforcer was Eugene Ciasullo, a mob associate with connections to Mafia bosses in several cities. He was greatly feared as the brightest and most capable of Cleveland's mob soldiers loyal to John Scalish and Jack Licavoli.

Raised on the tough streets of East Cleveland,

Eugene decided that mob life offered more money and excitement than the lathing and plastering trades he had learned from his uncles. His entry in the underworld was via thefts and burglaries with men like Butchie Cisternino, with whom Eugene became very close. Later the two got into the loan business "renting" money for 5 percent weekly. If the loan amount was $1,000, then the borrower had to pay $50 weekly in "vigorish," or interest, until the entire principal was repaid. Cisternino and Ciasullo's system of renting money would be copied by loan sharks across the country.

Ciasullo was notorious for his hair-trigger temper. Though his gap-toothed smile would light up his face, anger him and he revealed a very dark side, a natural ferocity accentuated by intimidating, sharklike eyes. Eugene's fury could be awakened simply by someone interfering in an argument between him and a girlfriend, insulting a friend of his, or cutting him off on the road. The result would be merely another statistic: a bloodied and/or battered victim of Eugene's meaty hands, or maybe a nearby weapon like the old bladed lathing hatchet he kept under his car seat. On one occasion it was a cue ball that Ciasullo used to inflict numerous skull fractures during a bar fight. That particularly brutal attack prompted an F.B.I. agent to dub Ciasullo "the Animal."

Thus, Ciasullo attracted the attention of high-ranking Cosa Nostra members. He quickly became a busy and effective Mafia enforcer. On occasion, requests came in to John Scalish for the Animal to take care of a "headache" for another mob family. By the time John Scalish died in 1976, Ciasullo was suspected of numerous mob murders and vicious assaults across the country. But not once was enough evidence uncovered to indict him, let alone convict him. By the seventies, he and Butchie Cisternino had emerged as the leaders of a group of young Collinwood thieves and burglars who were dubbed the "Young Turks" by the local media. These men included Joseph "Joe Loose" Iacobacci, Alfred "Allie" Calabrese, and Joe Bonariggo.

If John Nardi was going to take over as Mafia boss, he needed his own crew and enforcer. He approached Eugene Ciasullo and told him his plans. But Ciasullo's loyalty was to Jack Licavoli and he refused Nardi's offer. It was a refusal that would cost him dearly.

So John Nardi went to Danny Greene. He didn't care if his crew would be Irish. He wanted to be the boss.

"Your enemies are my enemies," Nardi told Greene. "Let's fight them together."

Danny agreed. He was making some money with Nardi in the vending machine industry, but now he had an opportunity to be at the top.

Since he was the nephew of Little Italy's Tony Milano, the Cleveland mob's consigliere emeritus, Nardi felt he was entitled to a cut of the gambling at the upcoming Little Italy Feast of the Assumption. He approached Leo Moceri and demanded a percentage. If Moceri refused, Nardi would move in on his gambling operations in Akron.

"Keep your hands off the Akron rackets!" Moceri yelled. "And get rid of Danny Greene."

"I'll do what I damn well please!" Nardi countered.

"Do you know who I am?" Moceri screamed. "I'm Leo Moceri, and nobody pushes me around!"[2]

After hearing of the argument, Licavoli was quite disturbed. He would have to show John Nardi and Danny Greene that he was in charge. Tony Delsanter encouraged him to have both men murdered. Licavoli wanted to avoid a war, so he waited. Nardi and Greene didn't.

TWELVE

I T was 1:00 in the morning on July 21, 1976, and there was no warning. Eugene Ciasullo had just exited his Lincoln Mark IV and was walking up his front porch steps. When he reached the top, a small bomb, concealed in a flowerpot in front of the door, exploded. Eugene was struck in the stomach with dozens of concrete nails that had been packed in the flowerpot as shrapnel. The blast slammed Ciasullo into his front door, which collapsed inward. He struggled to his feet but didn't enter his house for fear of jeopardizing his family's security. Instead, Eugene pulled a .38-caliber revolver from his waistband and ducked into the darkness of his backyard. His would-be assassin might move in to finish him off. Though critically wounded, Ciasullo hoped to be waiting.

By then the two bombers, rumored to be a Greene associate and a member of the Hell's Angels, were almost to their car, parked on the opposite side of a wooded area across from Ciasullo's home. With one arm tucked firmly against his side to control the bleeding, Eugene hopped numerous fences, making his way to the home of an uncle. He banged on the door, and within a few minutes an ambulance was racing Ciasullo to a nearby hospital.

Word of the bombing spread quickly through the ranks of the Cleveland Mafia. Butchie Cisternino and his crew were devastated. If Greene could do this to Eugene, then they were all in grave danger.

At the hospital, X-rays showed that dozens of nails had ripped into Eugene's intestines, stomach, and gallbladder. He wasn't expected to last the night, but still Butchie Cisternino and other crew members stood guard outside his room, declining an offer of police protection.

Amazingly, Eugene's condition improved. For two weeks his mother came daily to sit at his bedside. There she knit and prayed for her son. Though Cisternino or another of Ciasullo's friends was always outside the door, working in shifts to guard Ciasullo, Eugene kept a revolver stashed in his mother's knitting bag.

Eugene had surgery in which his gallbladder and part of his intestines were removed. His condition improved but it would be slow going. After two weeks in the hospital, he flew south and took up residence at his Florida home to recuperate.

After a few weeks, Cisternino begged Ciasullo to return and rejoin the war against Danny Greene. Eugene was upset that Butchie had asked him to return after he had almost been killed.

He demanded that Cisternino and the others kill someone themselves; then he'd return.

In the meantime, John Nardi and Danny Greene continued their offensive. Only weeks after mob enforcer Eugene Ciasullo was bombed, underboss Leo Moceri received a threatening phone call.

"Leo, you're dead," the unidentified caller said.[1]

Leo's girlfriend expressed concern over the call, but Leo laughed. "If anyone wanted to kill me I wouldn't get a call about it," he told her. "They would just do it."

Two weeks after the phone call, Moceri disappeared. Several days later his Mercedes was found abandoned. In the trunk were his golf clubs, lying in a pool of blood. Moceri's body was never found.

More violence followed as Danny Greene sent out members of his Celtic Club to eliminate potential competition in the rackets and settle old scores. On one evening, police arrested Keith Ritson and Kevin McTaggart. The men were cruising around the west side in a vehicle that was camouflaged to look like an unmarked detective's car. Ritson and McTaggart had a pistol, a shotgun, and several maps in their possession. Circled on the maps were locations of the homes of several of Greene's targets, including Eugene Ciasullo, Allie Calabrese, and Joseph B. Kovach Jr., former Teamster and employee of a prominent firechasing company.

In the meantime, news of Leo Moceri's murder buzzed through the twenty-four Cosa Nostra families in the United States. That a family underboss could be killed by outsiders was a major embarrassment to the Cleveland mob.

"Nardi's the brains behind it," Tony Delsanter suggested to Jimmy Fratianno. "This guy's gone fucking crazy since Johnny Scalish died.

You know, he was never made and it really pissed him off. They took Leo out first—he's the one they feared the most. Now we've got a war on our hands."[2]

"You guys need some soldiers," Jimmy said. "How long since you've made anybody?"

"Oh, shit, Scalish never made nobody for years and years. We need some young guys, new blood, some good workers."

"How about Ray Ferritto?" Jimmy suggested. "He's a good man. Want me to give him a call?"

"You know, Jimmy, he's a good friend of Ronnie Crab—Ronnie Carabbia. In fact, we had Ray at Mosquito Lake for one of our Fourth of July bashes. Yeah, give him a call. I'd like to talk to him."

Tall and thin, with salt-and-pepper hair, Raymond Ferritto was a bookie and professional burglar from Erie, Pennsylvania. Raymond had entered the world of crime quite early. At age thirteen he was convicted of burglarizing two gas stations and was sentenced to two years of probation. During his twenties, Ferritto was a bookmaker and vending machine route man in Erie. He was married in 1948 and fathered three children before he divorced in 1956. He remarried in

1957 and had one child. By that time Ferritto had moved to Warren, Ohio, where he met Ronald Carabbia and Tony Delsanter. Carabbia was one of three brothers, all known as "Crab," who had become prominent in Youngstown-area organized crime. Delsanter was a made Mafia member and associate of the Licavoli family. He managed the Cleveland mob's gambling interests in the Mahoning Valley.

By the late sixties, Ferritto had moved to Los Angeles, where he was associated with a group of Cleveland hoods that included Julius Petro. In the forties, Petro wriggled free from a death sentence on a retrial in a murder case. Ferritto and Petro were associates of Jimmy Fratianno, who by that time was on his way up the ranks of the Southern California Mafia. Likewise, Ray Ferritto was trying to make a name for himself.

In 1969, Petro was involved in a conflict with a well-known and successful Los Angeles bookmaker who used him as muscle. The bookmaker wanted Petro dead. He hired Ferritto and an accomplice, a burglar from Cleveland, because they disliked Julius.

Ferritto tried to plant a bomb on Petro's car. While assembling the explosive, Ferritto accidentally detonated the blasting cap, causing a minor injury to his leg. He opted for the "one-way ride" execution next.

Ferritto booked a flight from Los Angeles to Erie. He was driven to the airport by the accomplice, who enticed Petro to go along for the ride. The accomplice wheeled the car into an airport parking garage spot. Ferritto waited for a plane to take off, thrust a gun to the back of Julius Petro's head, and pulled the trigger. The single fatal report was muffled by the roar of the jet. Petro's killing went unsolved for years, until a dramatic turn of events began to unfold.

In 1971, Ferritto was convicted of burglary, this time with explosives. He was sentenced to fifteen years and incarcerated at California Penal Institution for Men (in Chino). Jimmy Fratianno also happened to be doing time at Chino and the two became friends. In 1974, Ferritto was released from Chino and returned to Erie. He started bookmaking again and also worked for a vending company that was owned by a cousin. By that time Ray had developed an ulcer serious enough to require partial removal of his stomach. To calm his nerves, he took handfuls of antacid tablets and even smoked marijuana.

In May of 1976, Ferritto received a call from Jimmy Fratianno. Ferritto drove to Warren, Ohio, to meet with Fratianno in the cocktail lounge of a motel. Fratianno was with a West Coast insurance agent paying $5,000 to meet with Jackie Presser. The three exchanged greetings and the insurance agent left.

"They're having some problems in Cleveland," Fratianno explained. "Somebody's trying to muscle in. I think you should talk to Tony [Delsanter]. You might be able to make some money with him."

Ferritto said he was interested, but wanted to know what was in it for him.

"Well, if you're interested I can set up a meeting with Tony and you can talk about it then," Fratianno said.

Two weeks later Fratianno telephoned Ferritto in Erie and arranged a meeting. The next evening Fratianno, Ferritto, and Delsanter met at Cherry's Top of the Mall Restaurant in Warren.

"You guys got business to take care of," Fratianno said. "I'll see you later."

Jimmy walked over and sat at the bar. Ferritto and Delsanter sat down at a table, exchanged amenities, then lowered their voices to just above a whisper.

"Has Jimmy told you about the problems we're having with Ray?" Delsanter asked.

"Just that somebody's trying to muscle in on the gambling."

"There's two," Delsanter explained. "John Nardi and Danny Greene, and they've gotta be taken care of."

"I'm interested, Tony, but what's in it for me?"

"I'll have to ask Jack because he's the boss."

Greene was too big a prize for an exclusive murder contract. In the beginning, Ferritto was unaware that other attempts were being made to kill Greene and Nardi. They had become such a nuisance to Licavoli that numerous mob associates were interested in killing them. It was assumed that the successful assassin would be greatly rewarded and gain instant respect in the underworld. Ferritto didn't hear from Carabbia or Delsanter for several months. In the meantime, the situation in Cleveland's underworld was approaching chaos.

BEFORE FERRITTO COULD ACCEPT THE CONTRACT to kill Greene and Nardi, Butchie Cisternino and convicted bank robber Allie Calabrese would attempt to kill Nardi at the behest of Jack Licavoli.

It was September 10, 1976, and Nardi was saying goodbye to friends and relatives at the Italian-American Brotherhood Club in Cleveland's Little Italy. On Tuesdays, the exclusive club featured elaborate dinners attended by judges, politicians, and prominent businessmen and presided over by Tony Milano, now ninety years old. It was just past 10:00 p.m., but the area was well lit by street lights. A hundred yards down Mayfield Road—past the popular Italian restaurants, bakeries, bars, and the Holy Rosary Church—Cisternino, Calabrese, and an associate acting as a sniper were concealed on a railroad bridge overlooking the neighborhood. They watched the front of the Italian-American Brotherhood Club. As John Nardi reached to unlock the door of his brand-new Buick, the gunman squeezed off his first round. The sharp report sliced through the traffic noise from nearby Euclid Avenue, but the sniper's aim was off slightly.

Nardi ducked behind the car as several more shots followed. One smashed through the driver's door. Two more shattered the windshield. After a few moments of wary silence, keeping his head down, Nardi crawled through the passenger door and over the crumbled glass, put the key in the ignition, and sped off.

Another attempt was made a few days later when a shotgun blast was fired at Nardi from a moving car. When reporters received tips about the shootings, they sought out Nardi for comment. He denied a rumor he was feuding with Licavoli.

"I'm not feuding with anybody," Nardi said with a laugh in a *Cleveland Press* interview. "That's ridiculous. Why would I feud with Jack White? The man is a friend of mine. I've known him all my life. Besides, what would we feud about? I could see if there was a million dollars in this town, but there isn't. What are you going to take over? Headaches?"

Nardi also denied that Danny Greene worked for him.

"We're just friends. I'm friends with everybody." Nardi was asked about friends and associates reputed to be in the Mafia. "The newspapers say they're in the Mafia. I don't know that. I never ask anybody their business."[3]

In the meantime, Nardi's word on the street was quite different from the story he gave the reporter. There was indeed something to feud about. Whoever succeeded in taking over the Cleveland

Cosa Nostra throne would inherit control of the billion-dollar Teamsters pension fund and thousands monthly from the Las Vegas skim and local gambling operations.

"Five of them guys are gonna go," he told an associate. "And you're going to be reading about it in the newspaper."[4]

After learning of the murder attempts on Nardi, Ray Ferritto phoned Ronnie Carabbia to find out what was happening with the plans they had made. Another meeting was set up and again Ferritto drove to Warren. Tony Delsanter, Ronnie Crab, and Butchie Cisternino were there, along with a new face, John Calandra, a close friend of Licavoli's.

The men shook hands and sat down for a short meeting over dinner.

"I've read there have been attempts on John Nardi. Is the deal still good?" Ferritto asked.

"It's still good," Calandra answered.

"Ray, we've had problems getting a schedule on Greene and Nardi," Delsanter added. "Their moves are erratic and we can't pin them down."

"There's been a lot of people calling about Leo," Calandra said. "They want to know what's happening and if anything's being done."

The meeting ended with an agreement that Ferritto would assist in trying to track down Greene.

Two weeks after Nardi was shot at, Greene's men wired a bomb to the ignition of Allie Calabrese's Lincoln Continental. Calabrese lived on a quiet street in Collinwood and made a habit of parking his car at a neighbor's house, since he didn't have a driveway. He left his key in the car in case it had to be moved. Up until this time, the mob's war with Danny Greene had been without innocent casualties. That ended when Calabrese's fifty-year-old neighbor, Frank Pircio, got up to leave for work. Calabrese's car was blocking Pircio's, so he hopped in the Lincoln to move it and was killed in a horrific explosion.

Not only were bombs being used in the Mafia war with Nardi and Greene, but they had become a favorite weapon in northeast Ohio gangland. Cleveland was dubbed "Bomb City, U.S.A." by a *Cleveland Press* reporter. The Bureau of Alcohol, Tobacco and Firearms was so inundated with blast investigations that they tripled their manpower in northeast Ohio.

"If they do nothing else, they make people sit

up and pay attention," Edward Whelen wrote for *Cleveland Magazine*:

> For, while Americans are becoming inured to street violence (whether they accept it or not), bombings, with their God-awful terror and indiscriminate destruction, retain their power to startle and shock—the last frontier of violence. A bombing is the ultimate violent act intended to kill, maim or war . . . A bombing provokes headlines, regardless of the human or property destruction, because the act itself appears so aberrant and the possible shredding of flesh—innocent flesh—is so real.[5]

A month after Frank Pircio was killed, Ronnie Carabbia telephoned Ray Ferritto and arranged another meeting at Cherry's Top of the Mall Restaurant. The next evening Ferritto drove to Warren, where he met with Tony Delsanter, Jack Licavoli, Butchie Cisternino, and Carabbia.

The men exchanged greetings, took a table in the bar area, and spoke softly.

"Jack, Ray's interested but he wants to know what's in it for him," Delsanter explained.

Young Danny Greene in his St. Jerome baseball uniform. As a child, Danny was a poor student who misbehaved often, but his skill on the field won him the support of the teachers and staff at his Catholic school. It wasn't until high school, when Danny began getting into frequent fights, that he was expelled, the reason for which is recorded as excessive tardiness.

Collinwood was the proud neighborhood for a proud Irishman.

Danny Greene, as he appeared in his Marine Corps induction photo. After graduating high school in 1951, Danny joined the U.S. Marines. Promoted to the rank of corporal in 1953, he trained new recruits as artillerymen because of his own excellence in marksmanship. Danny received an honorable discharge later that year.

Danny Greene in his first known mug shot. Over the course of his life, Danny not only eluded law enforcement efforts to put him behind bars but also outsmarted his fellow mobsters, dodging many attempts on his life.

Leo "Lips" Moceri. The feared Cleveland mob underboss and cousin to James Licavoli was the victim of one of Danny's kill orders. This particular 1976 murder shocked the Cleveland, and its thirst for revenge became even stronger.

Frank Brancato. Brancato was one of the senior Mafia members who brought Danny into the Cleveland mob scene by taking the kid under his experienced wing.

The headquarters for Local 1317 of the International Longshoremen's Association as it appeared in the 1960s. The HQ stood nearby the old Cleveland Stadium.

The "shape-up." Dockworkers who hoped for work would gather on any given day outside Danny Greene's ILA local HQ.

Danny Greene questioned by journalist Sam Marshall. Marshall collected affidavits that proved charges of extortion against Danny, causing him to be exiled from the union and convicted of embezzlement. The conviction was later overturned on appeal and Danny pled guilty to falsifying union records, after which he was charged a $10,000 fine and given a shorter prison sentence. However, Danny never paid a dime and did not spend a day in prison for the offense.

Eugene Ciasullo. Known as "the Animal," Ciasullo was the Mafia enforcer and first casualty in the Cleveland mob's war with Danny Greene and John Nardi.

Shondor Birns. This mug shot shows Birns, the former Cleveland Public Enemy Number One, after his 1957 arrest. A handwritten update (shown) was incorporated by a detective after Birns was killed by a car bomb planted by Danny Greene.

Birns was blown in two and out the roof of his Lincoln Continental. His upper torso (facedown) and foot (partially socked) with heel are shown in this police photo. Birns' murder marked the start of the Irishman's war against the Cleveland family.

John Nardi. Danny allied himself with John Nardi, a union official and reputed mob boss candidate, after breaking off from the Cleveland family to start his own gang, the Celtic Club. Together, Danny and Nardi were responsible for taking out a number of mob boss James Licavoli's supporters, including "Lips" Moceri.

Celtic Club business card. Members of Danny's Irish-American gang, the Celtic Club, were given names of famed Celtic warriors and frequently quizzed on Irish history. They were also supplied with business cards— green ink on a white background—and pens with green ink.

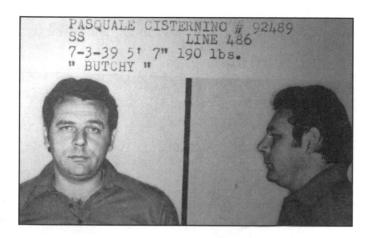

Pasquale Cisternino. More often known as "Butchie," Cisternino was the mob soldier who led the Cleveland Mafia's efforts to eliminate Danny and John Nardi and, with them, the Celtic Club.

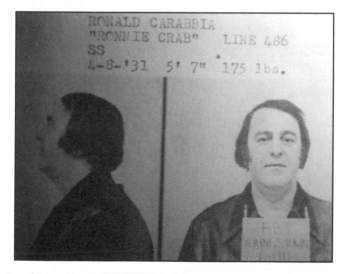

Ronald Carabbia. Born in Youngstown, Ohio, Ronnie Carabbia was one of the Cleveland Mafia men who would finally succeed in killing Danny.

A replica of the car door bomb box used in Danny's murder was constructed by police and used in court to convict his assassins.

The actual bomb box set used to kill Danny was designed to direct the blast, thus maximizing its killing power. Constructed by Mafia soldiers, the bomb was planted in the bushes near the front entrance to Danny's girlfriend's apartment. Its use was abandoned because it was feared elderly residents who paused at the entrance to chat would be injured.

Danny Greene, shirtless and sporting his gold Celtic cross, looks more like a Celtic warrior than ever.

Overhead shot of the Greene murder scene taken by the Lyndhurst Fire Department's ladder truck. The bomb car is shown on the left next to the Lincoln that Danny was getting into. His body is visible under the right rear corner of the bomb car.

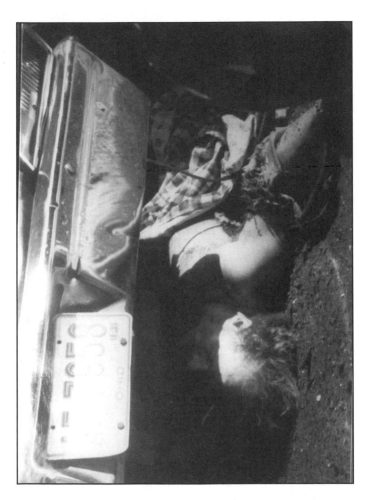

Danny's body lies under the rear of the bomb car used to kill him. Finally the Mafia had won their war with the Irishman. Or had they?

James "Jack White" Licavoli. This mug shot was taken after the Mafia boss was arrested for his role in Danny's murder.

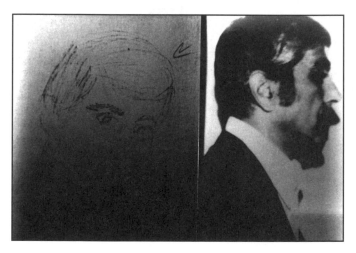

Ray Ferritto mug shot and sketch. This drawing of Ferritto, made by an eyewitness, was used to identify him only days after the murder as one of the Mafia associates retained to kill Danny.

Keith Ritson. One of Danny's chief enforcers for the Celtic Club, Ritson was involved in the attempted murder of Eugene Ciasullo and the killing of Leo "Lips" Moceri. Ritson was so feared that the Mafia offered to end the war with Danny if he sacrificed Ritson. But of course Danny refused.

After Danny's death, Ritson joined the Zagaria drug ring and ended up working for the very people who wanted him dead. Ritson's body was later pulled from an Ohio quarry.

Never publicity shy, Danny Greene poses for a newspaper photo shortly after the 1975 bombing of his apartment in Collinwood.

"Don't worry, Ray, we'll take care of you," Licavoli promised. "We can pay you one lump sum or we could make you. If you'll go to Detroit, we'll make you and give you 25 percent of the Warren and Youngstown gambling profits. You won't have to worry about money for the rest of your life."

"Okay, when you're ready, call me," Ferritto said.

"In the meantime, Butchie will do the legwork," Licavoli added. "And if a chance comes up to get Ritson and McTaggart, hit them too."

As casually as that, the decision was made. Licavoli now had a proven killer to take care of the Irishman.

THIRTEEN

I N April of 1977, an explosion jolted the residents of Collinwood awake. When police and fire units arrived, they found a white male lying dead next to a burning car. The body had massive damage to the head; it was obvious that the man had been at the focus of the blast. The bomb had been planted on the car of Mafia associate John Del Zoppo. But further investigation revealed that the dead man was not Del Zoppo. It was a Hell's Angel by the name of Enis Crnic. Crnic had reportedly been retained by Danny Greene to murder Del Zoppo. Either Crnic had detonated the bomb accidentally, or someone with him had set it off purposely. Only the person or persons in the red car witnesses saw speeding from the scene could answer that question—but they were never identified.

Crnic's death posed a major problem for the Hell's Angels. For some time, the Mafia had been using the Angels as muscle, but now the Cleveland mobsters were furious. It was obvious that the bikers also accepted murder contracts against them. Jack Licavoli issued stern warnings to local Hell's Angels members, and his men held a meeting attended by the club's president. The biker boss defended his club by explaining that it was not responsible for Crnic's actions because he was a former member at the time he planted the bomb. Despite distrust and finger-pointing by mob members, the explanation was accepted by Licavoli. But it was two years before the Hell's Angels were used for another mob contract.

Instead, Licavoli decided to induct some new blood into his ailing outfit. Mafia protocol required that he get permission to make new members from the commission in New York. He approached Anthony "Fat Tony" Salerno of the Genovese Mafia in New York City. Salerno had been running things for boss Frank "Funzi" Tieri, who was ill. Since the thirties, the Cleveland family had had a good working relationship with the

Genovese family and was therefore represented by them on the commission. The Genovese family also represented the Buffalo and Pittsburgh Cosa Nostra families. Licavoli and Lonardo flew to New York and met with Salerno. They explained the problem with Greene and Nardi and received permission to make ten soldiers.

Back home, Licavoli inducted John Calandra and Anthony "Tony Lib" Liberatore during a ceremony in the downstairs room of a Little Italy restaurant. John Calandra was an unlikely figure to become a made member of the Mafia. Sixty years old and still working at his Collinwood tool and die shop, he was in poor health, as was the small white poodle he often toted around. His police record consisted of only one line, but he was a fiercely loyal friend to Licavoli. Liberatore, on the other hand, had spent two decades incarcerated at the Ohio Penitentiary and the London, Ohio, Prison Farm for his involvement in the 1938 murders of two Cleveland police officers. He was paroled in 1958 by an acting governor and became active in Laborers Local 860, where he quickly demonstrated his leadership abilities. In 1972 he was granted a full pardon, and in 1975, Cleveland mayor Ralph Perk appointed him to the Regional

Sewer Board. By then Liberatore had been elected as business manager for Laborers Local 860.

Liberatore wanted to move up the ranks of the Cleveland crime family quickly. A unique opportunity to impress Licavoli came to him, of all places, at a Christmas party.

Jeffery Rabinowitz, thirty-two, a high school dropout, worked as a car salesman at Cross Roads Lincoln-Mercury with Kenneth Ciarcia, an older salesman there. Stocky, with a dark complexion, Ciarcia was successful at Cross Roads thanks to his close friend Tony Liberatore, who sent him many customers.

Rabinowitz and his twenty-nine-year-old girlfriend, Geraldine Linhart, lived together and were to be married. Their plans for the future included a suburban dream house. But the purchase of the new home was being prevented by a land contract lawsuit filed against their existing house.

During a Christmas party for the dealership, Ciarcia made a point to meet Linhart. He had a keen interest in her because she worked as a secretary with the F.B.I.'s bank robbery squad. Ciarcia got Linhart alone and struck up a conversation with some comments about his inability to do people favors.

"You know, Gerri, I'm fed up with everything. I used to have a lot of contacts but now I can't even get my son-in-law a job," he complained.[1]

Linhart listened politely as Ciarcia rambled on for some time. Then his conversation turned to Jack Licavoli and Tony Liberatore.

"So what's going on at the F.B.I. with Jack White and Tony Lib?" he inquired boldly.

Linhart shrugged her shoulders.

"Why don't you check and see what you can find out?" Ciarcia suggested. "I'm sure they'd appreciate knowing. Maybe Tony could return the favor by helping with this civil case that Jeff told me about. Lib knows a lot of people."

The prospect of getting some inside influence with her land contract case appealed to Linhart. But she knew the risk of getting into trouble at work was too great. Ten days went by and Ciarcia telephoned Linhart suggesting again that she come up with something on White and Liberatore. Linhart refused. Ciarcia pressed on, promising that she would receive help with her case. The conversation ended with Linhart saying she'd think about it. A few days later, Ciarcia called her back. Linhart made their conversation brief and told him there were volumes of information.

Ciarcia pressed for more information, and the next day Gerri Linhart left her desk in the bank robbery squad, retrieved an investigative report on James Licavoli, photocopied it, and refiled the original. She wrote James Licavoli at the top. That evening she took the report copy to Ciarcia's house. He skimmed through and asked her about the numbers in the report.

"The numbers refer to informants," she explained.

"Can you find out who the informants are?"

"Why?"

"Well, we just want to find out who is talking about us."

"The F.B.I. uses numbers so the informants can't be identified," Gerri explained.

"What about this informant number 882SD?"

"The SD stands for San Diego but I would never be able to find out who that is," Linhart insisted. "I don't know what else I can do for you."

Ciarcia took the file, wrapped it in newspaper, then stuck it in an empty Froot Loops cereal box. The next day he took the box to work and placed it in a cupboard where he stored some of his personal belongings.

During the next few days, Ciarcia continued

to phone Gerri asking for the identities of the informants. He promised that, in return, her civil court case would be taken care of. Linhart was apparently growing more desperate about her case. A few weeks later, in an unprecedented breach of Justice Department security, she entered the top secret informant room of the F.B.I. and hand-copied a list of informants. The names were classified as "TE," or top echelon, the highest ranking of the federal informers. Among the names on the list were John "Curly" Montana, a suspected mob hit man, and Teamsters figure Tony Hughes. Another name on the list was Daniel J. Greene, the code name "Mr. Patrick" in parentheses.

Linhart was still having second thoughts. She kept the list without telling anyone while Ciarcia continued to call her. He promised that her court case was being taken care of and pressed for the informant information.

Finally, Gerri told Ciarcia that she did indeed have something for him. At his request she brought the list to Cross Roads Lincoln-Mercury, where Ciarcia and Tony Liberatore were waiting.

"Where's the list?" Liberatore asked her.

"I don't like this whole business," she said.

Lib tried to reassure her. "Nobody is going to get hurt. I know a lot of people. Your court case is going to be taken care of."

"I don't like this," she continued. "I don't like the position I'm being put in."

Liberatore got up. "I'll be right back," he said as he left Ciarcia's office.

A few minutes later he returned and offered Gerri $1,000 in cash. It was enough to ease her second thoughts. She took the money and gave Liberatore the stolen list of informants.

Liberatore copied the names onto a separate sheet of paper, then burned Gerri's original list. In late September, Linhart lost her court case. She complained to Ciarcia, who promised carpeting for the new house in lieu of their promise to fix the case. He arranged another meeting with Liberatore.

"We're here as a sign of good faith," Liberatore began. "You've been nice to us and we want to help you out."

Gerri told Liberatore she needed $15,000 for the new house

"I couldn't possibly give you that much money," Liberatore insisted.

"I never even wanted money, just to get my

court case settled favorably," she reasoned, striking a nerve with Liberatore.

"Meet me back here in the morning."

The next morning, Linhart was waiting when Liberatore arrived. He extended a bulging envelope toward Gerri.

"Okay, here's the money," he said. "You can pay me back when your old house gets sold."

Linhart wanted payment for her services, not a loan. But she was desperate. She reached for the envelope. Liberatore hesitated.

"I just want to know if you're good for it," he asked.

"I am," she replied.

It was a promise she would come to regret

FOURTEEN

FOR years, Danny Greene had been searching for that one big score to finally bring him lasting power and money. By now he knew he was a marked man, but he told friends he wasn't concerned.

"I'm going to make all the money I can while I'm still around," he once said.[1]

In 1976, the Drug Enforcement Administration had Greene under investigation for the suspected purchase of phenylacetic acid, which is used to manufacture methamphetamine, or "speed." According to the D.E.A. report, a company believed to be owned by Greene ordered 551 pounds of phenylacetic acid and paid with a bank check for $1,267.30. There had been a smaller order a year earlier, but it was canceled before delivery was made.

Apparently Greene had abandoned his original plans under the heat of the D.E.A. investigation. But in 1977, he and John Nardi thought they had struck gold. They began working on a joint venture in which they would take over a financially ailing cattle ranch in Texas and sell the meat to labor union members through a discount purchasing program. The ranch owner had been indicted but acquitted on charges of conspiring to sell explosives to Cuba. Heavily in debt, he was likely to go bankrupt. Nardi's underworld connections would be able to lock up the purchase. He'd arrange for the financing and Greene would be his point man.

The meat would be sold through cooperative outlets across the nation, and a laborers' union membership card would entitle Greene to a generous discount, a setup already used to provide union members with other discounted services or products, like medical insurance and eyeglasses. It would be a major moneymaker—and, better yet, legal. Relocating to Texas would also end their problems with the Mafia and free them from the bitter Cleveland winters. Danny was preparing for the move with some custom-made western wear—complete with green cowboy boots and hat.

Greene had Columbus attorney Donald Eacret form an umbrella company for the deal. It was to have a Gaelic name—Micuarata Corporation—meaning "mountain in which my treasures are stored." As usual in his dealings with lawyers, Danny never paid Eacret for his legal work: Danny claimed that the publicity attorneys received for representing him was compensation.

Eacret later said that the numbers would have never worked for Greene and Nardi.

"Greene and [the ranch owner] projected annual sales of $6 million over a five-year period," Eacret explained. "But it would have taken $7 million just to refurbish the feeder lot and plant. And that does not include buying new cattle."[2]

For the meat deal, John Nardi planned to seek financing from Paul Castellano, boss of the Gambino mob clan in New York City. Castellano had decades of experience in the meat industry. Tony Milano set up an appointment with Castellano for his nephew, and Greene and Nardi booked a flight to New York.

Their plans to relocate to Texas were not happening fast enough for La Cosa Nostra's taste. Butchie Cisternino got wind of the travel plans and rented a hotel room overlooking the parking lot at Cleveland Hopkins International Airport. Cisternino and an accomplice waited for Greene and Nardi to leave for New York, then planted a remote-controlled bomb on their car. It was a perfect setup. When Greene and Nardi returned from New York and got into their car, Cisternino and Calabrese would be watching from their hotel room window to trigger the explosive. With the press of a button, the Mafia's worst headache would be over.

On March 14, 1977, Nardi and Greene returned from their two-day trip. Butchie was watching with binoculars and spotted the two men walking toward Greene's car. He readied the remote control and laid his thumb gently on the button. Nardi went around to the passenger side and Greene unlocked the driver's door. When both men closed their doors, Butchie pressed the button.

Nothing. Butchie pressed the button again. Nothing. He pressed it numerous times. Still nothing. Nothing but the sound of a jet taking off and a view of Greene pulling out of the parking spot.

Butchie and his accomplice ran to the hotel stairwell and started quickly down the eight flights of steps while Greene cruised out of the lot, headed for the parking tollbooths. When they reached the ground floor, they opened the door to the lobby and ran toward the hotel exit as several curious bystanders looked on. Repeatedly, Butchie pressed the detonator. By this time Greene and Nardi were out of view and at the parking tollbooth. Butchie and his partner could only watch in dismay as their quarry escaped again.

In the meantime, Danny sent Keith Ritson and Brian O'Donnell to warn Nardi that Jack Licavoli had a contract out on him.

"Don't worry," Nardi said. "Jack is my friend. I've known him all my life."[3]

John Nardi was a devoted family man who enjoyed picking up his grandchildren after school and bringing them over for dinner. Those were his plans on May 17, 1977, after leaving his office that afternoon.

Nardi had been taking precautions. He carried a gun and had been parking his car in several different locations. Today it was in the rear of the Teamsters Joint Council 41 offices, across from the musicians' union. Assassins had located it earlier in the day and were waiting when Nardi reached to unlock his door.

The explosion of the vehicle parked next to Nardi's blew his legs off. Officials and members from the Teamsters' and musicians' union offices ran outside to help to pull him from the fire, smoke, and wreckage.

"It didn't hurt," Nardi whispered. He was pronounced dead minutes later.

Despite having Raymond Ferritto looking to kill Greene and Nardi, Jack Licavoli reportedly assigned hit man Curly Montana to hunt down Nardi. The F.B.I. maintained that Montana and another individual planted the bomb that killed Nardi. The bomb was reportedly prepared by Butchie Cisternino.

In the wake of John Nardi's murder, his family members refused to admit that he had any ties to organized crime.

"Johnny was always helping somebody," his uncle, Tony Milano, explained to a *Cleveland Press* reporter. "The F.B.I., the C.I.A., the police. The newspapers made him out to be somebody he wasn't. He was just a union man. He didn't bother nobody. He was no Mafioso."[4]

Nick Nardi, John's brother and a respected labor leader, added: "John's death is the direct result of news stories about him. The stories built him up to be somebody to get out of the way. He was not involved in anything. He was always helping people, getting them jobs."

Shortly after Nardi's murder, Danny Greene granted several interviews to television and newspaper reporters. He told a *Cleveland Press* reporter, "I have a message for those yellow maggots. That includes the payers and the doers. The doers are the people who carried out the bombing. They have to be eliminated because the people who paid them can't afford to have them remain alive. And the payers are going to feel great heat from the F.B.I. and the local authorities."

In an interview with WJW-TV reporter Bill McKay outside the Celtic Club, Danny was flanked by two of his men. He stood shirtless with his cross gleaming in the sunlight. His arms were folded defiantly, and he looked more like a Celtic warrior then ever. He answered McKay's questions confidently.

"Rumor has it, Danny, that the word was out

on the street back in March that John Nardi was a target," McKay said. "Did you talk to John Nardi at all about this?"

"I haven't personally seen John in about three and a half months, but I did send him a message very recently [saying:] John, be careful, it's out here very, very strong on the streets that somebody's out to get you. Now from what I can see is that everybody says they heard this also. The investigators should start right there and go from who told you and where did they hear it from."

"Do you have any thoughts about where these people are from?"

"I think most probably the bomb was made here—the people could have been imported."

"Word has it, Danny, that you are also a target in this so-called gangland war for control. What's your answer to that?"

"In the world of the streets I happen to have a very enviable position to many people because I'm in between both worlds, the square world and the street world, and I think I have trust in both sides. I have no axe to grind, but if somebody wants to come after me, I'm over here by the Celtic Club. I'm not hard to find."[5]

Licavoli, Calandra, and the rest of the

Cleveland Mafia hierarchy and their admirers were incensed. Did this brazen bastard have any idea of who he was dealing with? Did he have a death wish?

One week following Danny Greene's televised challenge to the Mafia, Tony Delsanter, the Cleveland mob's Youngstown representative, died unexpectedly. Jack Licavoli, Jimmy Fratianno, Butchie Cisternino, and Ray Ferritto attended the wake. Licavoli pulled Fratianno aside and showed him the stolen list of F.B.I. informants he had obtained from Tony Liberatore. The Weasel had good reason to be very nervous: for almost a decade, Fratianno had been an F.B.I. informant in California. He scanned the list.

"This is great, Jack. Can she get information like this from California? You know we've got some stoolies out there."

"I don't think so, Jimmy. Not unless it's got something to do with Cleveland."[6]

After the wake, the men went to dinner and discussed the situation. Licavoli told Ferritto that he was going to be getting tape recordings made from a tap that had been placed on Greene's girlfriend's telephone. Licavoli told Ferritto he'd see what he could do to get it to him. He also told him that if Ferritto was successful in killing Greene, then he would make him and give him 25 percent of their gambling money coming out of Youngstown and Warren.

When Fratianno returned to Los Angeles, he phoned his F.B.I. contact who worked out of the San Diego field office. He told him about the list of informants stolen from the Cleveland office. Fratianno just wanted him to contact the Cleveland agents to inform them of the leak. At first the agent didn't believe him.

"Check it out yourself," Fratianno urged. "Two of the names on the list were Tony Hughes and Danny Greene."

Hughes was Jackie Presser's right-hand man.

"If it's true, then it's an historic breach of F.B.I. security. There would be many people whose lives are in danger with a leak like that," the agent said.

"Yeah, no kidding. So just call them and have 'em plug the leak."

"Jim, it's not that easy. This could turn out to be very big. We'll need detailed information— you'll have to go back to Cleveland to get more for us. And eventually, you'll have to testify."

"No way."

Jimmy's F.B.I. contact was adamant about

Fratianno getting involved, but Jimmy continued to refuse. The agent forwarded the little information he had to the Cleveland agents. At first, they, too, could not believe there was such a monumental leak in their office, until they were provided with the names of Tony Hughes, Jackie Presser, and Danny Greene.

The Cleveland F.B.I. had a mole in their midst.

FIFTEEN

IN June of 1977, Raymond Ferritto drove his 1974 Cadillac from Erie, Pennsylvania, to Cleveland. It was the first of numerous trips that Ray would make to gather information about Greene. Licavoli had given him $5,000 in expense money through Ronnie Carabbia. Butchie Cisternino provided Ferritto with a list of license plate numbers and descriptions of cars that Danny used. He also gave him a *Cleveland Magazine* issue which contained an article entitled "The Bombing Business." The story included photographs of Greene and Nardi. Angelo Lonardo provided Ferritto with cassette tapes from the tap on Debbie Smith's phone.

For a time, Ferritto and Greene even lived in the same apartment building. During nervous drives in and around Collinwood, Cisternino showed Ferritto Danny's trailers on Waterloo, his girlfriend's apartment building on Lakeshore Boulevard, and the Kenny Kings Restaurant that Greene frequented. For months, Ferritto and either Butchie Cisternino or Ronnie Carabbia cruised Collinwood, trying to spot the Irishman.

But Greene remained an elusive target. He surfaced at last in an attempt to make peace with Licavoli. Danny made the cease-fire offer through Frank Embrescia, an aging senior mob member in ill health. Licavoli's terms were that Greene's lieutenant, Keith Ritson, be sacrificed for his supposed role in the murder of Leo Moceri and the attempted murder of Eugene Ciasullo. Danny refused.

Ferritto continued his surveillance, often parking across from the Lakeshore Boulevard apartment. On one occasion he observed Greene walking out of the building. On another he learned from listening to the telephone recordings that Greene would be at the Sheraton Motor Lodge on the east side. (Danny was holding a party for his girlfriend's family, visiting from out of town.) Ferritto drove there and observed Greene's car in the lot. But nearby was another car, with Greene's son and another man watching the area.

Believing that an atmosphere of peace might relax the cautious Irishman, Jack Licavoli reluctantly agreed to a plan devised by Jimmy Fratianno. The scheme would involve the Gambino soldiers who had loaned Shondor Birns the $70,000 that in turn was loaned to, and lost by, Greene. They, too, were interested in justice. A meeting was held between Fratianno, Licavoli, the Gambino soldiers, and Danny. It was decided that Greene could temporarily take over gambling operations on the west side of Cleveland. This would allow a cease-fire and also give Danny the opportunity to repay the loan from the Gambino family.

Shortly after the meeting, Greene and his men quickly moved in on a large west side gambling operation originally run by John Nardi. Danny offered Licavoli a percentage, but he declined. He didn't want money from Greene—he wanted him dead.

While Danny Greene let his guard down a bit, informal meetings to plan his murder continued, often at Butchie Cisternino's apartment in Collinwood. Allie Calabrese and Ronnie Carabbia would be there to discuss strategy. On occasion, John Calandra showed up carrying his white poodle.

In August, Ferritto met with Tony Delsanter and Jack Licavoli at the Living Room restaurant in Warren. Ferritto complained that he was using his own credit card for expenses, had no car to use, and wasn't getting much help from anyone. Licavoli was not one to part with his own money. He stalled, telling Ferritto he would see what he could do.

By early September, Ferritto and Cisternino decided on a plan of action. They would set up a remote-controlled bomb in the bushes near the front door of Danny's apartment and detonate it when Greene walked by. To increase the effectiveness of the explosive, Cisternino had a steel box constructed to direct the blast. The bomb would be placed in the box, which would be secured to the ground with railroad spikes, with the open side of the box facing the target area. The explosive itself included a large plastic jug filled with gasoline and nails to act as shrapnel.

Tony Liberatore was assembling a team of his

own to kill Greene. He retained two ex-cons, one of whom was a paroled killer. He provided them with guns and a car—ironically, an old police cruiser.

"If you pull this off, you won't have to worry about a thing," Liberatore promised the men. "This thing has gone on long enough. Jack White wants this done. You gotta get it done. You get this thing done and you can write your own ticket in this town."[1]

On September 24, 1977, the F.B.I.'s Title III surveillance equipment intercepted a conversation inside Licavoli's house:

LICAVOLI: Johnny Nardi. That cocksucker. And this fucking Irishman.

CALANDRA: How the hell did this guy ever come into the picture?

LICAVOLI: Everybody's around him. You can't get near him . . . If he says he'll be there at three o'clock . . . fuck it, who gives a shit. You wait, you wait and wait and then you get tired of waiting. He don't keep no time.

CALANDRA: He's no dummy.

LICAVOLI: Yeah, like the game that Nardi opened on the west side. Boy, did the Irishman want to give me a piece. I don't want nothin' from that sonavabitch.

CALANDRA: He's got to screw up some time.

LICAVOLI: Oh, he's got to make a mistake. I hope he goes back to Texas so they can kill him there.

CALANDRA: Where, Jack?

LICAVOLI: Texas. Them cocksuckers on the west side, they all go with him. You know, McTaggart and all them.

The following week, Ronnie Carabbia called Ferritto and told that something had come up. The two men met at Carabbia's vending machine company. From there they drove forty minutes to Mosquito Lake, a private boating resort and picnic area halfway between Cleveland and Youngstown. At the gate, they were greeted by Jack Licavoli, John Calandra, Butchie Cisternino, and Angelo Lonardo.

The men boarded an eight-sleeper luxury boat owned by a physician friend and went into the enclosed cabin. There they listened to a cassette tape recording made from the tap on Greene's phone. Of interest was a call made by Greene's girlfriend, confirming an appointment for him to get a loose filling repaired on October 6, 1977.

On Wednesday, October 5, 1977, Ray Ferritto drove to a suburban apartment owned by a friend of Butchie Cisternino. Cisternino was there and Ronnie Carabbia arrived an hour later. The three men walked outside and Cisternino showed them the "Joe Blow" car, a maroon Chevy Nova registered to a fictitious name and outfitted with a special steel bomb compartment welded into the passenger door. The three went back up to the apartment, where they talked, ate, and watched television into the evening.

The next morning Cisternino returned with a brown paper shopping bag. Inside the bag were a police scanner and the components to make the bomb: a nine-volt battery with alligator clips, blasting caps, the remote control detonator, and three sticks of dynamite wrapped in brown wax paper. Butchie laid the parts on the table and with Ferritto's help began carefully and methodically assembling the bomb. They finished in an hour.

The explosive and receiver were held in a cigar box with an inner switch to make contact when the remote control was triggered. There was also an outside safety switch to activate the whole package and prevent the possibility of an accidental detonation. The remote control detonator was actually a device used to fly model airplanes, an eight-inch-square plastic box housing a lever, a meter, and a telescopic antenna. Cisternino placed the assembled bomb in one shopping bag and the remote control in another.

At 2:00 p.m., an hour before Greene's scheduled dental appointment, Ferritto and Ronnie Carabbia left the apartment with the bomb car and the getaway car. Cisternino stayed behind to monitor the police radio. The afternoon sun shone bright and warm as the two men made their way south on Interstate 271, twenty minutes to Exit 32 at Cedar and Brainard roads in the bedroom community of Lyndhurst.

Carabbia pulled the bomb car into the parking lot of the six-story Brainard Place Medical Building and immediately parked it near the lot entrance. He got out and walked over to where Ferritto had parked the getaway car to get a good view of the whole lot and the main entrance. Carabbia got into the car with Ferritto and the two hit men began the wait for their target.

Fifteen minutes later, Tony Liberatore's

backup hit team arrived in their old police car, the emblem outline still visible on the door. The rifle supplied to them lay on the backseat, wrapped in the same piece of flowered cloth it was picked up in. A .357 Magnum revolver lay under the passenger seat. They pulled next to Ferritto and Carabbia and the men discussed what to do. It was decided that Liberatore's men would use the high-powered rifle to kill Greene. They moved their car to the opposite side of the parking lot, where they, too, would have a clear view of the main entrance.[2]

It was now 3:00 p.m., and Greene was nowhere in sight. At 3:15 p.m., Greene had still not shown up. Carabbia and Ferritto chatted about the likelihood that Greene had once again eluded them. For several months Danny had been switching cars with Keith Ritson as a tactic to avoid detection. But the backup team also saw Danny enter the lot, and readied their high-powered rifle. Danny steered the big Lincoln into a parking slot, then pulled forward into the adjoining empty space for an easy exit. He grabbed his green leather gym bag from the passenger seat. The bag was essentially a portable survival kit: inside was a Browning 9mm semiautomatic pistol capable of firing fifteen rounds without reloading, an extra clip of bullets, a list of car license plate numbers of several of Licavoli's soldiers, a box of green ink pens, and a Mother of Perpetual Help holy card.

Danny exited the car, locked the doors, and started walking quickly toward the building entrance. Greene's old friend Billy McDuffy was supposed to watch the Lincoln while Danny was at the dentist. Before he left for his dental appointment, Greene paged McDuffy, but he never got the message because the batteries in his pager were dead.

Danny was already twenty minutes late as he disappeared inside the lobby. A few minutes later, the backup hit team pulled up next to Carabbia and Ferritto. They said they didn't shoot because they thought there was somebody in another car watching Greene. Ferritto told them he and Carabbia would use the bomb car and that they could leave.

As the two backup men left, Ferritto pulled the bomb car through the lot and backed it in next to Danny's car so that it was facing the same direction. Ever so delicately, he placed the bomb package inside the steel bomb box along with a large package of nuts and bolts. Ferritto switched the remote control receiver on, replaced the steel box cover, and tightened down the nuts. He spread a green blanket over the top of the bomb box to hide it from outside view. Whether Ferritto and Carabbia chose a green blanket as a sarcastic joke or by accident, no one knows. Ferritto got back into the Plymouth with Carabbia and pulled out to the street, stopping off the road near a phone booth. They had a good view of the front entrance as they waited for Danny to exit the building.

Inside Brainard Place, Danny went to the third-floor office of Dr. Dominic Candoli and checked in with the receptionist. Danny left the office, took the elevator back down to the lobby, and walked to a pay phone. He called his son Danny Jr. with instructions to bring his eyeglasses to a restaurant in Collinwood, telling him he'd need them to sign the papers for the big meat deal.

Danny returned to Dr. Candoli's office and was ushered to a dentist's chair. The dentist worked on Danny for roughly fifteen minutes, chatting cheerfully as he repaired the loose filling. After Dr. Candoli completed the work, the two men said goodbye and Danny checked out with the receptionist.

Minutes later, Greene emerged from the building and walked toward his car. Ferritto hopped in the driver's seat of the Plymouth and Carabbia climbed in the back. With bomb transmitter in hand, Carabbia watched intently from the backseat as the Irishman approached his car. When Danny reached to unlock his car, Carabbia pushed the detonator, triggering the bomb.

The remote-controlled explosive had found its mark. The bomb car was demolished and the Lincoln was severely damaged. Standing only inches from the steel-box-encased bomb when it exploded, Danny Greene was killed instantly. There was much horrific damage to his back, but his body was left largely intact—except for his left arm, which was blown almost one hundred feet away, his prized emerald ring still attached to his finger.

Greene's body landed faceup just under the rear end of the bomb car. After at least five attempts on his life, the Irishman was dead. Like an impromptu memorial, his gold Celtic cross was embedded in the asphalt a few feet away. Danny would have said that he died proudly, without fear, facing the man upstairs. Danny's strings had finally been pulled and his coveted guardian angel had been powerless to intervene.

In the meantime, Ferritto and Carabbia's escape did not go unnoticed. Moments after the bomb exploded, a young woman and her husband noticed Carabbia ducking down in the backseat of the getaway car. Once on the interstate, the young couple took notice of the blue Chevrolet again as it passed them. This time there was no rear passenger.

As Ferritto passed by, the young woman got one quick look at his face. Lady luck was holding neither Greene's nor Licavoli's hand that day. The odds were probably a million to one, but Raymond Ferritto's mug had just been recorded in the alert mind of an artist. And being the daughter of a policeman, she was sharp enough to copy down the Pennsylvania license plate.

When the couple arrived home, the woman immediately telephoned her father and gave him the license plate number. Then she sat down and drew a sketch of the man driving the blue Nova. A mammoth investigation had just gotten off to a rocket start. The woman's father turned the sketch and license plate number over to investigators Andy Vanyo, Rocco Poluttro, and Ed Kovacic of the Cleveland Police Investigation Unit. Ferritto was already known in the C.P.D. Intelligence Unit and the sketch was such an accurate likeness that they were able to identify him immediately.

SIXTEEN

THE headlines screamed CAR BOMB KILLS DANNY GREENE. Television news programs repeatedly aired footage from the blast site, including grisly shots of the Irishman's severed arm. Greene's henchman Kevin McTaggart was interviewed.

"He wasn't afraid of dying," McTaggart said. "Danny told me, 'The Irishman's always a target. When it's your time, the man upstairs pulls your string.'"[1]

Several days after Greene's murder, the F.B.I. intercepted some interesting conversation through its "Title III" surveillance at mob boss Jack Licavoli's Little Italy house. Apparently Licavoli, his right-hand man, John Calandra; and

an unidentified male were complaining about
Greene's brazen behavior, and about mob fig-
ures Frank Embrescia, Frank Brancato, and John
Nardi. They felt that these men, as well as the
F.B.I., were responsible for the Irishman's rise to
power.

LICAVOLI: [Embrescia] was so fuckin' burned
up . . . If he couldn't handle him, that's his
own fault.

CALANDRA: That's right. That's right.

UNIDENTIFIED: How can a marked man put a big
flag in front of his house? He had a big Irish
flag out by the side, anybody could see it. He
put it there on purpose. He'd be sitting out
there under the sun.

CALANDRA: He has some pretty good connections,
though.

LICAVOLI: He had some connections, all right.
The fuckin' F.B.I. He used to tell them about
every goddamned thing everyone did.

CALANDRA: You know that with Greene. He was
the F.B.I.'s boy.

LICAVOLI: Oh, fuck yes. But he didn't work with
the F.B.I.; he told them what to do!

CALANDRA: Sure, you're right.

LICAVOLI: He said F.B.I. your ass. He thought he
    got so fuckin' big.

UNIDENTIFIED: Right.

LICAVOLI: Well, he wanted it all, that's all. Him
    and Nardi. That fucker. He used to give them
    the money and he used to give them all the
    information. They created a monster.

CALANDRA: Brancato?

LICAVOLI: That's right. They created that guy. And
    all the fuckin' headaches we used to have.

Licavoli didn't know it then, but his headaches were just beginning.

WHILE DANNY GREENE'S REMAINS WERE CREMATED
in a private service, one of the most effective and
far-reaching cooperative law enforcement efforts
ever had gotten under way. A strike force of
various agencies was amassed to solve the historic
Mafia hit. They included the Cleveland Police
Department; the Lyndhurst Police Bomb Squad;
the Federal Bureau of Investigation; the Bureau
of Alcohol, Tobacco and Firearms; the Cuyahoga
County Sheriff's Office, the Pennsylvania State
Police; and the U.S. Attorney's Office. The
Cuyahoga County prosecutor appointed two

attorneys to work exclusively with the strike force. It was a monumental case. Detectives of the Lyndhurst Police Department interviewed six hundred people.

Investigation began with the getaway car license plate number and was aimed at Raymond Ferritto. A check of license applications revealed that the bomb car and the getaway car bore sequential registration stickers. They had been applied for together and the applications had the same handwriting. The strike force now had the two cars linked together.

A search warrant was executed at Ferritto's house in Erie, Pennsylvania. Some interesting items were confiscated from the house, including the *Cleveland Magazine* issue containing Greene's photograph. But the most incriminating evidence was found in Ferritto's Cadillac. There, stuck in the visor, investigators located the registration papers to the getaway car.

An arrest warrant was issued for Ferritto. His photograph was flashed on television news shows and published in numerous Midwest newspapers. Concerned that he was being described as armed and dangerous, Ferritto surrendered to police in Pittsburgh and was extradited to Cleveland.

Raymond Ferritto waited patiently in jail, hoping that Licavoli would supply a good attorney for him. He hoped wrong. Instead, Ferritto got wind that there was a contract on his head. If the mob got rid of Ray, there would be nobody to testify against the others. Ferritto was appalled by their treachery.

"All my life I'd been one way," he later said during an interview for The Discovery Channel's *Crime Inc.* "I always did what I was supposed to do and now all of a sudden I did them the biggest favor that they wanted done and they were talking about killing me and here I am in jail awaiting trial."

The mob had forced his hand. Ferritto had only one way out. He made a deal with the feds.

"It wasn't because I saw God or read a Bible. It was just that I thought at that time that I had to look out for me . . . And I thought that would be my best move."

In addition to revealing everything he knew about the Greene murder plot, Ferritto was required to plead guilty to the 1960s murder of Julius Petro in Los Angeles. After several weeks of debriefing Ferritto and preparing affidavits, the strike force divided into teams to execute the warrants. Licavoli was arrested at home. His cane with the long hidden blade was immediately confiscated, along with $3,000 in cash agents found in the don's underwear drawer.

Angelo Lonardo was also apprehended at home. At his request, agents let him change his clothes for the trip downtown. He put on a suit and tie. His wife offered the agents coffee and cookies while they waited. They declined.

John Calandra was picked up at his Crown Tool and Die Shop in Collinwood. Butchie Cisternino and Allie Calabrese were both arrested without incident at their respective homes. Thomas Sinito was taken into custody at a friend's house.

In North Miami Beach, Florida, F.B.I. agents apprehended Ronnie Carabbia at a motel. He was registered there under the fictitious name of Crown, perhaps a reference to Calandra's tool and die shop. At the same time, F.B.I. Special Agent Jim Ahearn arrested Jimmy Fratianno in San Francisco.

In the meantime, Cleveland F.B.I. agents were still looking for leads in the theft of their files. They received a call from a man who refused to give his name. He said he thought he had something that belonged to the F.B.I. and wanted to meet with an agent. When F.B.I. agents met with the man, he handed them a grocery bag.

"I think this belongs to you. I put it back together just like I found it."[2]

The man was the owner of Cross Roads Lincoln-Mercury. Inside the bag was a cereal box. Inside the box was a stack of papers wrapped in newspaper. It was the stolen file on Licavoli.

"I was so happy I could've kissed the guy," the agent later said.

At F.B.I. headquarters, agents examined the file copy from Cross Roads. A handwritten notation on the first page was compared against dozens of samples from various F.B.I. employees. They got a match when they checked it against secretary Gerri Linhart's (now Rabinowitz, as she and Jeffery had married). The agents couldn't believe it. It was a bittersweet finding. They were fond of Gerri and thought of her as a most loyal and dedicated coworker. But fingerprint results confirmed it.

Before the agents approached Linhart, they salted their current list of informants. They took some names off and added other names of organized-crime figures who were not informants.

They hoped to create confusion with any underworld characters who viewed their list.

A few weeks later, the agents approached Linhart. They had barely begun questioning her when she broke down crying.

"I knew you guys would eventually get me," she sobbed. "I'm so glad it's over."[3]

In a plea bargain, Linhart agreed to cooperate with the F.B.I. and testify against Ciarcia and Liberatore. Arrest warrants were issued and Ciarcia was arrested. Liberatore could not be located and eventually was placed on the F.B.I.'s Ten Most Wanted Fugitives list.

SEVENTEEN

As the historic Danny Greene murder trial got under way, Raymond Ferritto testified that Butchie Cisternino detonated the bomb. Later he recanted his testimony.

"I was upset with Butchie for supplying me with a getaway car that could be traced," Ferritto explained.[1]

Ferritto was a star witness, but circumstances had produced an even more damaging turncoat. Jimmy Fratianno was already on the run from West Coast mobsters who correctly suspected him of being an informant. The charge of conspiring to kill Danny Greene put him over the edge. F.B.I. agents convinced him that the only way out was to join WITSEC and become a cooperating witness.

"I had two choices," Fratianno said. "Either cooperate with the government or stay out and get killed."[2]

It was an unprecedented success for law enforcement. Fratianno had decades of experience in the Mafia and had been close to many bosses. A $100,000 bounty was immediately placed on the Weasel's head. Fratianno's 1978 defection presaged the decline of the Italian-American Mafia.

The Greene murder trial was a marathon— seventy-nine days—making it the longest continuous criminal litigation in Cuyahoga County history. One hundred and twenty-nine witnesses testified. Four hundred pieces of evidence were presented to the jury, including replicas of the car door bomb box and the remote control bomb— wired to ring a bell and flash a light one hundred yards away from the explosion.

But in the end, only Cisternino and Ronnie Carabbia were convicted. Allie Calabrese had been discharged for lack of sufficient evidence, and all of the others were acquitted.

Cisternino's alibi failed him. A friend testified that he called Butchie from a certain phone booth during the time that Cisternino was supposed to be assembling the bomb. The friend told the court that Butchie was at home, making spaghetti sauce. The plan backfired when Sergeant Rocco Poluttro of the Cleveland Police Intelligence Unit checked out the phone booth that the call was allegedly made from. An investigation with Ohio Bell Telephone Company representatives revealed that the phone booth had not been installed until one week after the call was supposedly made. Cisternino's friend was convicted of perjury.

The confusing finding by the jury that Greene's murder was not part of an organized-crime battle also contributed to the acquittals. Lyndhurst police chief Roger Smyth couldn't figure it out.

"What was the jury thinking?" he asked reporters in frustration. "Do they think Carabbia and Cisternino killed Greene just for the hell of it? Certainly this was a murder for hire."

But Chief Smyth still looked on the bright side.

"I'm not going to say all our efforts were for naught. We did get Carabbia and Cisternino. We got Ferritto and Fratianno and [Liberatore's backup team] to plead guilty. We also got the Rabinowitzes, who stole some F.B.I. files, to plead guilty to helping the mob. And we got [a car dealer] to plead guilty to forgery. That's nine people convicted from one gang bombing."[3]

Had Chief Smyth known the damage coming to the Mafia—not only in Cleveland but nationally—as a result of Danny's murder, he might not have been so disappointed at the results of this first trial.

Cisternino's defense attorney was bitter over his client's conviction. "If they didn't believe it was a murder for hire with gangland overtones, then why convict anybody?" he argued. "If nobody paid to have this done, then what sense does it make to think that two men would kill Greene for no reason? It was a compromise verdict, plain and simple."[4]

One prosecuting attorney explained that the jury had trouble believing Ferritto and one of the backup hit men who flipped: both men were convicted killers. Other investigators were very sour that Licavoli and the other top mobsters weren't convicted.

One Cleveland Police detective, interviewed by a *Cleveland Press* reporter, lambasted the Cleveland Mafia.

"They could have killed Greene easily, often,

if they had just walked up to him with a shotgun and let fly . . . They didn't want to face him man to man. Danny would have scared them up a tree, even if he wasn't armed."[5]

"They just wanted to get off as cheaply as possible," an F.B.I. agent said. "I think their total cash outlay in this thing was $5,000. If the mob had brought in a real professional and done the job right it would have been another unsolved bomb killing. The Cleveland mob is cheap. That's all there is to it. There's money here, but they must all bury it in their backyards in tomato cans."[6]

JACK LICAVOLI DIDN'T HAVE LONG TO CELEBRATE his acquittal in the murder of Danny Greene. The strike force had prepared for the possibility of failure at the state level. Federal racketeering indictments were unsealed and he was arrested again in 1982, along with several mob associates.

"Danny Greene died five years ago and he's still fucking with us," a defense attorney groused.

Convicted of racketeering as a result of the federal charges were Licavoli, Ronnie Carabbia, John Calandra, and ten lower level gangsters. U.S. District Court judge William Thomas immediately revoked Licavoli's $400,000 bond.

When the sentencing hearing came up, punishment was stiff. Licavoli was given seventeen years and immediately shipped off to the Oxford, Wisconsin, Federal Correctional Institution. He later complained that the Wisconsin dampness aggravated his arthritis.

After numerous months on the F.B.I.'s Ten Most Wanted list, Tony Liberatore was finally arrested in Cleveland, where he had been hiding at a friend's home. He would be convicted of his role in bribing F.B.I. secretary Geraldine Linhart and sentenced to twelve years.

Joseph Griffin, special agent in charge of the Cleveland field office, was delighted.

"This is the first time in the FBI's campaign against organized crime that we've taken out the entire leadership structure of a major La Cosa Nostra family," he said.[7]

Several months after the federal trials ended, Raymond Ferritto agreed to a paid interview for a *Crime Inc* Mafia special to be aired on cable television's Discovery Channel. The following is an excerpt from the exchange:

INTERVIEWER: How did you feel after you killed Greene? Were you elated?

FERRITTO: I was elated because the job was done and I was gonna become one of them and share in the profits. Something that, since I was a kid, I dreamed of, I wanted. And this was my chance to do it.

INTERVIEWER: Well, how does it feel to kill someone that you know every living breath of because you're tapping his phone, you're living in the same building with him? What's it like to have a man as a target?

FERRITTO: Well, to me it was like having a glass of wine. It didn't mean a thing to me. I killed him and there was no remorse that I killed a man because that was part of my life. I was brought up all through my life believing that those, you just have to put them out of your mind, those were things, hurdles that you had to overcome. A man with a conscience doesn't last long on the street.

Despite a penalty of death for betraying omertà, Ferritto never showed any fear:

INTERVIEWER: The Mafia has sworn to kill you. What is your comment?

FERRITTO: I know that I am as capable of taking

care of myself as the guy they send to take care of me. And it's just a matter of time for me. I'd be a fool to say that it isn't. Sooner or later they're gonna get me.[8]

And while Ferritto was talking to *Crime Inc*, the underworld intelligence sparked by the Danny Greene case continued to flow. After the trial ended, U.S. Marshals began hauling silver-haired Jimmy Fratianno around the country to testify in major mob cases. One of the first was the R.I.C.O. trial of Frank "Funzi" Tieri, boss of the Genovese mob group in New York. Tieri was convicted and sentenced to ten years. And as damaging a federal cooperating witness as Jimmy Fratianno was, there would be another man who would cause even more harm to the Mafia.

EIGHTEEN

NOT long after the Greene trial ended, Angelo Lonardo's lieutenants, Joey Gallo and Tommy Sinito, became involved in a large drug operation run by west sider Carmen Zagaria. Reportedly, Gallo and Sinito had Lonardo's blessing. A burly ex–high school football player who became a carpenter, Zagaria later bought his own floor-covering company. His ambition and business acumen could have served him well had he stayed in that field, but in the seventies he began dealing drugs on a small scale. In 1979 he bought a tropical fish store called the Jungle Aquarium, which served as a meeting place and front for his narcotics operations. At home, he kept a Doberman pinscher for protection. He named the dog Al Capone II.

After the death of their leader Kevin, McTaggart and Kevin Ritson joined the Zagaria drug ring. In a strange twist of events, they became associates of the same men they had been fighting. Ritson's involvement didn't last long: in late 1978, he disappeared and was presumed dead.

Carmen Zagaria's chief enforcer was a greatly feared German-American named Hartmut "Hans" Graewe. Graewe delighted in dismembering his victims to discourage easy identification. Nicknamed "Doc" and "the Surgeon," he kept a hacksaw and butcher knife in a bag and referred to them as his "tools." His car, an old Volkswagen van, was his "ambulance."

By 1980, the Zagaria-Gallo drug operation had grown to include at least twenty couriers. They were paid $1,000 plus expenses per trip and flew into Florida by commercial aircraft. While in Florida, the drug runners rented cars and paid for all expenses in cash to avoid the paper trail created by credit cards.

The Zagaria-Gallo partnership was making a fortune. But all of that money wasn't enough to avoid resorting to murder. There seemed to be no end in sight for the violent killings. In a two-year period, seven men were murdered as a result of clashes with Zagaria, Gallo, and Graewe. One significant case was Joseph Giaimo.

Giaimo was a drug wholesaler who worked out of a hotel he owned in North Bay Village, Florida. He was closely associated with the Cleveland Mafia family and mobsters in Florida and New York City. Joey Gallo instructed Zagaria to make his wholesale drug buys from Giaimo whenever possible.

In 1980, Carmen Zagaria purchased ten 1,500-pound loads of marijuana, 13 pounds of cocaine, and 600,000 Quaaludes from Florida supplier Joe Giaimo. But dealing with Giaimo became increasingly difficult because he was cheating on his drug sales. Zagaria accused him of using too much packaging paper or wetting down the marijuana, both methods of inflating the weight. Giaimo also substituted candy tablets for significant numbers of Quaaludes.

Despite Zagaria's mistrust of Giaimo, the two men began socializing and became friends. Giaimo told him of grievances he had with Sinito and Gallo. Zagaria reported to Sinito and Gallo that Giaimo wanted to cut them out. Sinito and Gallo were angry and started talking about killing Giaimo. The men decided to murder Giaimo but first planned to steal a shipment of drugs from him.

In early January of 1981, Zagaria sent a convoy of drug runners to Florida to pick up 1,900 pounds of marijuana from Giaimo. On the evening of January 17, Giaimo agreed to meet Zagaria at the fish store to get paid for the marijuana. When he got there, he and Zagaria started arguing. Giaimo became suspicious and drew a revolver from his waistband.

Hans Graewe had been hiding in the fish store. He sneaked up on Giaimo and shot him several times in the back of the head. Giaimo died instantly.

Zagaria didn't think he could get Giaimo's body out of the store without being noticed, so he and Graewe decided to dispose of the body right in the basement of the fish store. Using brick and mortar, they actually sealed the body into a wall, building a makeshift crypt. Eventually they removed the body to a secluded pond outside of Cleveland.

In the meantime, Joey Gallo continued his

attempts to recruit Zagaria into the Mafia. He believed that Carmen's ambition would bring new life to the Cleveland family. Gallo explained to Zagaria how mob chief John Scalish had failed to bring in new blood during the sixties and seventies. The result was a lack of experienced, strong leadership.

"See, there should be, like, people between us," Gallo said on an F.B.I. wiretap. "Know what I mean, Carmen? But they didn't do nothing for all those years over here. Just let it go dormant . . . See, Angelo [Lonardo is] probably one of the most respected guys in the whole United States . . . He's really the kind of guy we needed in this town a long time ago . . . But he's gonna be seventy. We're missing the guy that's sixty. And we're missing the guy that's fifty. It's all the way down to me at forty. That hurts us, see?"

Gallo told Zagaria that he expected to take over leadership of the family and that Tommy Sinito would be second in command. He told Zagaria he could join them and be in charge of a crew of soldiers. Zagaria said he was involved deep enough and didn't want to join the Mafia. But Hans Graewe thought this would be a good opportunity for his boss to take over everything and actually proposed killing all of the Cleveland Mafia members, starting with Licavoli and Lonardo.

During the time that Angelo Lonardo took over the Cleveland Mafia, law enforcers were closing in fast and hard on the Zagaria-Gallo drug operation. The haphazard killings, use of drugs by gang members, disorganization, and lack of discipline aided the F.B.I.'s two-year investigation of the $15-million-a-year drug ring. The investigation utilized room bugs, phone taps, and heavy surveillance.

In March of 1982, the multimillion-dollar operation came to a halt when Zagaria was convicted of selling drugs. He was sentenced to ten to thirty years in prison, but while free on bail he became a fugitive. He lived out of state, secretly returning several times to see his family. On September 23, he returned to Cleveland, called the F.B.I., and told them to meet him at Holy Cross Cemetery. There, beside his mother's grave, Zagaria gave himself up. She had died while Zagaria was on the run, and he had not been able to come back to pay his respects.

Facing the original conviction and sentence, additional federal drug charges, weapons charges, and potential indictments against members of his family, Zagaria followed the route that Ferritto and Fratianno had taken and became a cooperating witness for the federal government.

With his near photographic memory, Zagaria would prove quite damaging to his former crime associates. His testimony would result in the indictments of Angelo Lonardo, Joey Gallo, Hans Graewe, and Kevin McTaggart for vast narcotics dealings and almost one dozen murders.

In his debriefing, Zagaria cleared up the mystery surrounding the disappearance of several men, including Danny Greene's former lieutenant, Keith Ritson. In April of 1978, Ritson and Hans Graewe had a falling-out over a cocaine deal. Graewe believed that Ritson had cheated him. In August, an associate of Zagaria gave Ritson $2,500 to murder a drug dealer who had begun cooperating with police. Ritson had been drinking heavily and taking drugs. He kept the money but never committed the murder. Distrust and paranoia had become strong in the drug ring. When Zagaria approached him, Ritson revealed that he had several targets he wanted to kill, including his old buddy from Danny Greene's gang, Kevin McTaggart. Ritson's drug use continued to increase, resulting in unstable behavior that Zagaria and Hans Graewe considered too much of a risk. For several months, they discussed killing him.

On November 16, in the rear of Carmen Zagaria's fish store, he and Graewe sat with Ritson discussing drug business. Graewe got up and walked away. A few moments later, he returned quietly. In one quick motion he placed a .38 revolver to the back of Ritson's head and pulled the trigger. Zagaria flinched as Ritson instantaneously collapsed in his seat. Zagaria was upset: he hadn't planned on killing Ritson in his store.

Ritson's body shifted and dropped to the floor, breaking one arm of the chair. Graewe slipped a kitty litter box under Ritson's head to catch the spurting blood.

They wrapped the body in a canvas sheet and plastic, secured it with heavy chain, and dumped it in the same pond where they later disposed of Joe Giaimo's corpse.

Immediately after Zagaria flipped, he provided authorities with the location of Ritson's body.

NINETEEN

ANGELO Lonardo is probably one of the most respected guys in the whole United States . . ." said mob lieutenant Joe Gallo one day. "He's really the kind of guy we needed in this town a long time ago, but you know, nobody ever listened to him because . . . he don't express himself. But out of everybody that's left, this guy commands a lot of respect. One thing I know is people, and he is a beautiful person. Besides that, he's my boss, you know, but forget that, because I've had a lot of people that ain't worth the powder to blow them away. I respect him not only because I have to [but] because, I'm telling you, he's a great guy."

The conversation, secretly recorded by the F.B.I., would come back to haunt the mob and Joe Gallo in more ways than one.

Indeed, Gallo was right: Lonardo was greatly respected nationally by many of the most powerful Mafia leaders. And his quiet nature, typical of the old-school Mafiosi, was a form of protection against such traitorous members of the brotherhood like Jimmy Fratianno.

Even some police detectives and F.B.I. agents had a certain respect for Lonardo.

"To me, he was almost like the movie version of the Godfather," a policeman commented. "He was always the gentleman, not a tough street rat. He was someone who recognized us as people in the same general line of work—on an opposing team, of course."

And Lonardo maintained respect for the police. When detectives would arrive at his home to execute a search or arrest warrant, Lonardo and his wife would treat them like guests, even inviting them to sit and have coffee.

Strike force prosecutor Donna Congeni was impressed with Lonardo's demeanor in the courtroom. She was subjected to cruel, obscene insults from some of the other defendants and even their attorneys. But Lonardo treated her with respect and courtesy, even standing when she approached the defendant's table.

"He was the epitome of class," she once remarked.[1]

But Congeni was just as determined to send Lonardo away for life as she was the others. The task proved challenging.

"Because of his years of careful training in the art of secrecy and insulation, with meetings held in back rooms and decisions made with nods and coded phrases, our case against Angelo Lonardo was difficult to prove," said prosecutor Congeni. "But once informant Carmen Zagaria testified about Lonardo's methods, the jury could see his power and control."[2]

As a result of sentences handed down by U.S. District Court judge John Manos, Kevin McTaggart, Hans Graewe, Joey Gallo, and Angelo Lonardo would be destined to life behind federal bars. In a separate trial, Tommy Sinito pleaded guilty and was sentenced to twenty-two years in prison.

It had been a career proving crime pays. For decades, Big Ange Lonardo survived the most hazardous pitfalls of Mafia involvement: mob bullets and prison. Through fifty years of acquiring power and money through criminal and legitimate enterprises, he had spent only eighteen months incarcerated, and that was for the boldly executed vendetta that avenged the untimely loss of his father and launched his life in La Cosa Nostra.

F.B.I. agents had been visiting Lonardo and offering deals since his conviction in 1983. They promised to get him out of prison on an appeal bond. No doubt it was a tough decision. The mob sentence for violating omertà is death.

In August of 1983, Lonardo was brought to Kansas City to testify before the U.S. grand jury investigating skimming from several Las Vegas casinos. Lonardo refused to address questions alleging that he transported skimming proceeds between Chicago and Cleveland. Despite an offer of immunity and a judicial order, he would not betray omertà.

But back in his lonely cell at the U.S. Penitentiary in Lewisburg Prison, Lonardo must have been weighing his options. Perhaps life away from his family, his Cadillac, and his beautiful house was too much to give up. It was only after his first judicial appeal was denied that he picked up the F.B.I. agent's business card and quietly slipped away to a prison pay phone. He had made a painful decision that would have far-reaching effects throughout the national underworld.

"Are you still there?" he quietly asked.

Indeed, the F.B.I. agent knew what Lonardo meant. He was swiftly removed from Lewisburg and placed under twenty-four-hour guard, and the long process of betraying his past began.

When the word spread, Lonardo's relatives and friends couldn't believe it. They were shocked. If Danny Greene was watching, no doubt he was beaming at the chaos his war with La Cosa Nostra had sparked.

In the underworld, gangsters from New York to Los Angeles were reflecting on past dealings with Lonardo, nervously wondering what he might reveal. Fifty years of high-level Mafia knowledge was surely going to hurt a lot of people. It started with someone once very close to Lonardo. Several days before Lonardo's defection was made public, eighty-one-year-old Jack Licavoli was removed from the Federal Correctional Institution in Oxford and admitted to a local hospital. He had suffered a heart attack and would die five days later. Licavoli had been a quiet and ordinary prisoner.

Angelo Lonardo's defection was a grand

prize—a coup for the F.B.I. Joseph Griffin, then agent in charge of the F.B.I. field office in Cleveland, must have been delighted.

"Jimmy Fratianno was a captain. Joseph Valachi was a mere soldier," he explained to the news media. "Lonardo is to Fratianno and Valachi what the president of General Motors is to a foreman and an assembly line worker."[3]

After weeks of debriefing, legal procedures, and judicial technicalities, Angelo Lonardo, known appropriately in F.B.I. files as "Top Notch," was ready.

The first stop was back to Kansas City, where prosecutors had been unhindered by Lonardo's previous refusal to talk. They had returned indictments and the historic "Strawman II" skimming trial was under way. Among the defendants was Angelo's once-dear brother-in-law and companion, Maishe Rockman. Seated in the witness chair, seventy-four-year-old Lonardo looked aged and weary. But his testimony was effective. In addition to Rockman, numerous mobsters were convicted of skimming more than $2 million from two Las Vegas casinos. They included Joseph Aiuppa, boss of the Chicago Mafia, and Frank Balistrieri, Milwaukee's head mobster.

Following the trial, Jimmy Fratianno was used as an F.B.I. witness during the detention hearings. He provided key testimony used to incarcerate Aiuppa and the others without bail pending sentencing. Fratianno also testified that it was Aiuppa who ordered the murder of West Coast mob boss Johnny Roselli in 1976.

Lonardo spent the next three years in other federal courtrooms and before the U.S. Senate Permanent Subcommittee on Investigations, revealing everything he knew about the mob's operations. During an exchange with Senator Sam Nunn, he instructed the committee on the difference between a gang and a Mafia family:

SENATOR NUNN: You mention the murder of Leo Moceri. Who committed that murder?

LONARDO: I believe it was Danny Greene and Keith Ritson.

SENATOR NUNN: Why was that murder committed?

LONARDO: Well, Leo Moceri and John Nardi did not get along, and one day during the feast that they hold in Cleveland every year, in Mayfield—I think you know about that—Leo Moceri told John Nardi to mind his own business and he had better start behaving or otherwise he was going to get it. He says, "You know I'm the underboss now." He says, "Don't forget."

SENATOR NUNN: How was that murder carried out?

LONARDO: Well, John Nardi was being tried in Miami on narcotics and while he was there he gave Danny Greene the order, the contract to try to get Leo Moceri.

SENATOR NUNN: Was that murder carried out by the other gang, another gang—

LONARDO: Yes.

SENATOR NUNN [CONTINUING]: Against a member of your gang?

LONARDO: Against a member of our gang? No. He was a member of our family.

SENATOR NUNN: And someone from another family carried out the contract on him?

LONARDO: It was not a family. It was Danny Greene and Keith Ritson.

SENATOR NUNN: Did they belong to any kind of family at all? Was there any kind of—

LONARDO: They were what you call a gang.

Lonardo's knowledge of the underworld was brought from the Las Vegas skimming trial in

Kansas City to New York City. There, in September of 1986, he and Jimmy Fratianno were key witnesses at the *United States v. Salerno* trial. Dubbed the "commission case," this highly publicized and successful attack on organized crime began in 1980, when the New York City F.B.I. initiated an ambitious assault on the Mafia.

Strike force teams were assigned to build R.I.C.O. cases against each of the five Mafia clans in New York. The operation included New York State Organized Crime Task Force investigators, N.Y.P.D. detectives, and U.S. attorneys. Six years of investigation were capped by indictments of numerous high-ranking mobsters, including the bosses who made up the elite Mafia ruling commission. The case was dubbed "Star Chamber" by the investigators. In all, there were thirty-seven counts of loan-sharking, labor payoffs, extortion, and racketeering.

In addition to Clevelanders Angelo Lonardo and Jimmy Fratianno, the prosecution had celebrated F.B.I. agent Joseph Pistone on their side. Under the assumed name of Donnie Brasco, Pistone had gone undercover and infiltrated the Bonanno crime family. His historic penetration of La Cosa Nostra's inner circle netted a wealth of invaluable intelligence that provided an in-depth look at the structure and operations of New York City's five Mafia families. The commission case defendants included crime bosses Fat Tony Salerno, Carmine "Junior" Persico, and Anthony "Tony Ducks" Corallo. They were given life sentences.

Gambino crime family boss Paul Castellano had also been indicted but, prior to the trial, was killed in a plot led by his cocky lieutenant, John Gotti. Gotti, dubbed "the Dapper Don" because of his impeccable appearance and "the Teflon Don" because of his numerous acquittals, took over the Gambino family after Castellano's murder. Gotti eventually received a life sentence for the Castellano conspiracy.

In the meantime, the Justice Department had decided to remove Jimmy Fratianno from the WITSEC payroll after ten years of service. During his tenure as a federal cooperating witness, Fratianno commissioned author Ovid Demaris to write his biography, *The Last Mafioso*, and coauthored another book, *Vengeance Is Mine*, with journalist Michael J. Zuckerman. Later Fratianno sued Demaris, claiming that the book contained false quotes. He blamed the criticism of WITSEC in

Vengeance Is Mine for his being dropped from the witness protection program.

The Justice Department said it had spent $1 million protecting Fratianno—a figure that Jimmy disputed. A spokesman said that any further payments would make WITSEC look like a pension fund for aging mobsters. It was agreed, though, that Fratianno would continue to receive protection in dangerous areas.

Jimmy was still bitter. "They just threw me out on the street," he complained. "I put thirty guys away, six of them bosses, and now the whole world's looking for me."

Despite the Mafia contract on his life, his removal from WITSEC, and several appearances on national talk shows, Fratianno lived another six years until his natural death in 1993. He was seventy-nine.

EPILOGUE

"I T is very ironic," said F.B.I. agent Joe Griffin. "During his life, Danny Greene always tried to take out the Cleveland Cosa Nostra. He was never able to do it. In his death, he did."

Consider that, as a result of Raymond Ferritto flipping, Jimmy Fratianno became a prized cooperating witness for the Federal Bureau of Investigation. Together, his and Ferritto's testimony dismantled most of the Cleveland Cosa Nostra hierarchy. To regain their power and money, the Cleveland mob became involved in drugs, and as a result underboss Angelo Lonardo was sentenced to life in prison. He flipped and, at the time, was the highest ranking mobster ever to betray *omertà*. His and Fratianno's testimonies were used across the country in unprecedented convictions of major Cosa Nostra family bosses, which resulted in the fall of the Kansas City, Milwaukee, and Cleveland Mafia families.

Once it was apparent that the United States government could protect major Mafia witnesses, the option of trading information for freedom appeared more attractive to gangsters facing lengthy prison sentences. In the years following Danny Greene's murder, many powerful cooperating witnesses followed the path Fratianno and Lonardo had taken, including Luchese soldier Henry Hill; Vincent "Fish" Cafaro, right-hand man to Genovese boss Tony Salerno; and Philadelphia Mafia underboss Phil Leonetti. The most recent celebrated Cosa Nostra turn-coat was Gotti underboss Sammy "the Bull" Gravano.

Indeed, Danny Greene's most important legacy was in his death, the fallout from which devastated a once-mighty crime family and sparked events leading to a parade of Cosa Nostra defectors. Their secrets would be crucial to the government's success in the national war against the Mafia. Danny would have been proud.

Some day he'll die, as all we must,
Some will laugh but most will cry.
His legend will live on for years,
To bring his friends mixed pleasure.

—FROM "THE BALLAD OF DANNY GREENE"

ENDNOTES

Chapter 1
1 Interview with Ed Kovacic, Dec. 6, 1995.
2 *Cleveland Plain Dealer*, May 13, 1975.

Chapter 3
1 Interview with Sister Barbara Eppich, Order of Saint Ursula, Aug. 7, 1995.

Chapter 6
1 Interview with Skip Ponikvar, March 31, 1995.
2 *Cleveland Plain Dealer*, Sept. 15, 1964.

Chapter 7
1 Interview with Skip Ponikvar, March 31, 1995.

2 Interview with Ed Kovacic, Dec. 6, 1995.

3 *Cleveland Plain Dealer*, Oct. 4, 1987.

4 Ponikvar interview.

5 File notes of Faith Corrigan.

6 Most of the quotes regarding the grain boat operation come from Sam Marshall's exposé as reported in the *Cleveland Plain Dealer*, Sept. 13–23, 1964.

7 *Cleveland Plain Dealer*, Sept. 15, 1964.

8 Ponikvar interview.

9 *Lake Country News Herald*, Sept. 18, 1964.

10 *Cleveland Plain Dealer*, Sept. 18, 1964.

11 Interview with Mairy Jayn Woge, March 28, 1997.

Chapter 8

1 *Cleveland Press*, Nov. 5, 1971.

2 *Cleveland Press*, Nov. 27, 1971.

3 Cleveland Heights P.D. File A42046, Bombing death of Arthur Snepeger.

4 Interview with Susan Daniels, April 25, 1995.

5 Cleveland P.D. Report No. 71162, Frato Homicide, Oct. 5, 1972.

6 *Cleveland Press*, Oct. 5, 1972.

7 *Cleveland Plain Dealer*, Jan. 11, 1972.

Chapter 9

1 *Cleveland Magazine*, Nov. 1990.
2 *Cleveland Plain Dealer*, April 1, 1975.
3 Interview with Ed Kovacic, Dec. 6, 1995.
4 Kovacic interview.
5 *Exit* magazine, July 16, 1975.

Chapter 10

1 Interview with confidential source, July 15, 1995.
2 *Cleveland Press*, May 12, 1975.
3 *Cleveland Magazine*, Aug. 1978.
4 Interview with Ed Kovacic, Dec. 6, 1995.
5 Conversations with Greene's neighbor Patty: Interview with confidential source, Aug. 7, 1995.

Chapter 11

1 Austintown P.D. Report No. 1-1805, John Conte Homicide, Sept. 19, 1975.
2 *Cleveland Magazine*, Aug. 1978.

Chapter 12

1 Akron P.D. Report of Missing Person/Possible Homicide, Leo Moceri, Sept. 24 and 26 1976.
2 Exchanges between Delsanter and Fratianno,

about Ferritto Carabbia: *The Last Mafioso* by Ovid Demaris (New York: Times Books, 1981) and Ferritto's testimony in *State of Ohio v. Pasquale Cisternino, et al.*, Cuyahoga County Case No. CR-34326.

3 *Cleveland Press*, Oct. 22, 1976.

4 *Mobbed Up* by James Neff (New York: Atlantic Monthly Press, 1989).

5 *Cleveland Magazine*, April, 1977.

Chapter 13

1 Exchanges between Rabinowitz, Ciarcia, and Liberatore: Rabinowitz' testimony to the F.B.I. in field office reports 92-2748 and CV 183-231.

Chapter 14

1 *Cleveland Plain Dealer*, May 13, 1975.

2 *Cleveland Magazine*, Aug. 1978.

3 Ibid.

4 *Cleveland Press*, May 19, 1977.

5 WJW-TV News, May 1977.

6 Fratianno's conversations with Licavoli and his F.B.I. handler: *The Last Mafioso* by Ovid Demaris.

Chapter 15

1 F.B.I. affidavit of S. A. Kahoe, March 1978.

2 The account of Greene's murder is primarily from Raymond Ferritto's testimony in *State of Ohio v. Pasquale Cisternino, et al.*, Cuyahoga County Case No. CR-34326.

Chapter 16

1 *Cleveland Plain Dealer*, Oct. 8, 1977.

2 *Cleveland Magazine*, 1978.

3 F.B.I. 92-2748 and CV 183-231.

Chapter 17

1 Testimony of Ferritto in *State of Ohio v. Pasquale Cisternino, et al.*, Cuyahoga County Case No. CR-34326.

2 *New York Times*, March 20, 1980.

3 *Cleveland Press*, May 26, 1978.

4 Ibid.

5 Ibid.

6 Ibid.

7 *Cleveland Magazine*, Oct. 1982.

8 *Crime Inc*, Thames Television, Aug. 1, 1984 (Season 1, Episode 3), viewed on The Discovery Channel.

Chapter 19

1 *Cleveland Magazine*, Dec. 1985.
2 Ibid.
3 Ibid.

Epilogue

1 *Cleveland Plain Dealer*, Oct. 4, 1987.

SOURCES

Books

Allen, Edward J. *Merchants of Menace: The Mafia*. Springfield, IL: Charles C. Thomas, 1962.

Anastasia, George. *Mob Father*. New York: Zebra Books, 1993.

Delaney, Frank. *The Celts*. Boston, MA: Little, Brown, 1986.

Demaris, Ovid. *The Last Mafioso*. New York: Times Books, 1981.

Ehle, Jay C. *Cleveland's Harbor: The Cleveland-Cuyahoga County Port Authority*. Kent, OH: Kent State University Press, 1996.

Fox, Stephen. *Blood and Power: Organized Crime*

in 20th-Century America. New York: Penguin Books, 1989.

Giancana, Sam and Chuck. *Double Cross: The Explosive, Inside Story of the Mobster Who Controlled America*. New York: Warner Books, 1992.

Jacobs, James B., with Christopher Panarella and Jay Worthington. *Busting the Mob: The United States vs. Cosa Nostra*. New York: New York University Press, 1994.

Kobler, John. *Capone: The Life and World of Al Capone*. New York: G. P. Putnam's Sons, 1971.

Lavigne, Yves. *Hell's Angels: Into the Abyss*. New York: Lyle Stuart/Carol Publishing Group, 1996.

Maas, Peter. *Underboss: Sammy the Bull Gravano's Story of Life in the Mafia*. New York: Harper-Collins, 1997.

———. *The Valachi Papers*. New York: G. P. Putnam's Sons, 1968.

Messick, Hank. *The Silent Syndicate*. New York: Macmillan, 1967.

Messick, Hank, and Goldblatt, Burt. *The Mobs and the Mafia*. New York: Ballantine Books, 1972.

Neff, James. *Mobbed Up: Jackie Presser's High-Wire Life in the Teamsters, the Mafia, and the FBI*. New York: The Atlantic Monthly Press, 1989.

New American Bible (St. Joseph Edition). New York: Catholic Book Publishing, 1970.

Place, Robin. *The Celts: Peoples of the Past*. London: MacDonald Educational, 1977.

Porrello, Rick. *The Rise and Fall of the Cleveland Mafia*. New York: Barricade Books, 1995.

Ressler, Robert K., and Tom Shachtman. *Justice Is Served*. New York: St. Martin's Press, 1994.

Roemer, William F. Jr. *The Enforcer*. New York: Donald I. Fine, 1994.

Van Tassel, David D., and John. J. Grabowski, editors. *The Encyclopedia of Cleveland History*. Bloomington, IN: Indiana University Press, 1987.

Zuckerman, Michael J. *Vengeance Is Mine*. New York: Macmillan, 1987.

Magazine/Newspaper Articles

Aikens, Tom, Richard Gazarick, and Debra Erdley. Three-part series on the lives of the late Samuel and Gabriel "Kelly" Mannarino, *Pittsburgh Tribune-Review*, June 2–4, 1996.

"Come Home, Jack White," *Cleveland Magazine* ("Inside Cleveland"), Dec. 1984.

Drexler, Michael. "Default: The Real Story," *Cleveland Edition*, Dec. 15, 1988.

"Cleveland as a World Port," *Inland Seas* magazine, Fall 1948.

Kobler, John. "Crime Town U.S.A.," *Saturday Evening Post*, March 9, 1963.

Maas, Peter. "Who Is the Mob Today?" *Parade*, in *Akron Beacon Journal*, Feb. 25, 1996.

Magnuson, Ed. "Headhunters," *Time*, Dec. 1, 1986.

Marshall, Samuel F. "Probe of Daniel Greene and Local 1317 of the International Longshoremen's Association," *Cleveland Plain Dealer*, Sept. 13–26, 1964.

Murphy, Kim "The Godfather's Son," *Los Angeles Times*, Sept. 17, 1989.

Neff, James. "Can the Mafia Make a Comeback?" *Cleveland Magazine*, Aug. 1989.

———. "How the Mob Edited Your Morning Newspaper," *Cleveland Magazine*, Nov. 1989.

O'Donnell, Doris. "Theatrical Grill," *The Times of Your Life*, Holiday Issue, 1995.

Robb, David. "Hollywood Heavy," *L.A. Weekly*, July 7–13, 1995.

———. "Public Enemy Shondor Birns," *Cleveland Magazine*, Nov. 1990.

Roberts, Michael D. "Why They Blew Shondor Birns Away," *Cleveland Magazine*, date unknown.

Romano, Lois. "Jim Traficant, Wild Man on the Hill," *Washington Post*, April 23, 1990.

Rowan, Roy. "The Biggest Mafia Bosses," *Fortune*, Nov. 10, 1986,

Sciria, Paul. "Babe," *La Gazetta Italiana*, May 1995.

Sheridan, Terence. "The Death of Shondor Birns and the Rise of Danny Greene," *Exit*, July 16, 1975.

———. "High Life," *Cleveland Magazine*, Aug. 1988.

"Traficant Owes Back Taxes; Konnyu in Trouble at Home," *Congressional Quarterly* ("Inside Congress"), Sept. 19, 1987.

Trebilcock, Bob. "Mean Streets," *Ohio Magazine*, Jan. 1980.

Whelen, Edward P. "The Life and Hard Times of Cleveland's Mafia—How the Danny Greene Murder Exploded the Godfather Myth," *Cleveland Magazine*, Aug. 1978.

———. "The Lonardo Papers," *Cleveland Magazine*, Dec. 1985.

Wolf, Richard. "Ohio Lawmaker Takes to TV," *USA Today*, March 1990.

Newspapers

Akron Beacon Journal
Cincinnati Post
Cleveland Plain Dealer

Cleveland Press
Lake County News Herald
Los Angeles Times
New York Times
Pittsburgh Post-Gazette
Pittsburgh Press
Sun Newspapers
The Sunday Paper (Lake-Geauga)
Warren Tribune Chronicle
Washington Post
Youngstown Vindicator

CABLE TELEVISION

The Discovery Channel: *Crime Inc*, Thames Television, Aug. 1, 1984 (Season 1, Episode 3, "Racket Busters")

FEDERAL GOVERNMENT DOCUMENTS

Organized Crime Strike Force File on the Danny Greene Murder Conspiracy

Federal Bureau of Investigation Files
Field Office File 92-2748 and Bureau File 183-1331 (Danny Greene Murder Conspiracy)

F.B.I. affidavit of S.A. Michael Kahoe 3-78

F.B.I. affidavit of S.A. Thomas Kirk 3-78

F.B.I. affidavit of S.A. Robert Friedrick 11-77

F.B.I. affidavit of S.A. Michael Kahoe 12-77

F.B.I. affidavit of S.A. Robert Friedrick 10-77

F.B.I. affidavit of S.A. George Grotz 1977

F.B.I. intercepted conversations from the residence
of James Licavoli pursuant to court-ordered Title
III wiretap surveillance 1977

Frank Milano File-F.O.I.P.A. request file number
92-3229

Drug Enforcement Administration Files
Shondor Birns
Daniel J. Greene
Keith Ritson

United States Senate Permanent Subcommittee
on Investigations of the Committee on
Governmental Affairs
Profile of Organized Crime: Great Lakes Region,
Jan. 25–31, 1984 (Testimony of Peter Cascarelli)
Hearings on Organized Crime, "Twenty-five Years
After Valachi," 1988 (Testimony of Angelo A.
Lonardo)

United States District Court for the Western District of Missouri

U.S. v. Carl Deluna et al. (Testimony of Angelo A. Lonardo)

STATE GOVERNMENT DOCUMENTS

Ohio Organized Crime Investigations Commission, 1993 Status Report, Pennsylvania Crime Commission, 1976 and 1992 reports

Attorney General, State of California, Organized Crime Reports to the California Legislature

Cuyahoga County Common Pleas Court

Greene Murder Conspiracy Case Numbers 036324 (Testimony of Raymond Ferritto), 038130, and 042044

LOCAL GOVERNMENT DOCUMENTS

Akron, Ohio, Police Department. Report of Missing Person/Possible Homicide: Leo Moceri, Sept. 24 and 26, 1976

Austintown Township, Ohio, Police Department. Homicide Report: John Conte, Report No. 1–1805, Sept. 19, 1975

Cleveland, Ohio, Police Department. Homicide: Mike Frato, Complaint No. 71162, Oct. 5, 1972

Cleveland Heights, Ohio, Police Department. File A42046: Bombing death of Arthur Snepeger

Euclid, Ohio, Police Department. Bombing Death Report of Enis Crnic, April 5, 1977

Lyndhurst, Ohio, Police Department. Homicide Report of Daniel J. Greene, Oct. 6, 1977

OTHER

File notes of Faith Corrigan, retired *Cleveland Plain Dealer* reporter

APPENDICES

LA COSA NOSTRA

Organized Crime (OC) in the United States in the 1980s included four specific sectors of La Cosa Nostra: Cleveland, Pittsburgh, Southern California, and Kansas City. Even today, La Cosa Nostra is perhaps the most significant OC threat in the country.

Each sector had its own hierarchy, including a boss, underboss, consigliere, captains, lieutenants, soldiers, and others. They often were divided even further into groups by region. The following pages list the alleged and reputed members, associate members, and associates of each of the four above-mentioned sectors.

THE CLEVELAND
COSA NOSTRA*
Circa 1980

Boss: James "Jack White" Licavoli
Underboss: Angelo "Big Ange" Lonardo
Consigliere: John "Peanuts" Tronolone

Maishe Rockman

**Capos or Captains, Lieutenants,
Soldiers, and Others**

Eugene "the Animal"
Ciasullo
Butchie Cisternino

Carmen Basile
John Calandra
Jimmy "the Weasel" Fratianno
Tony Liberatore
Joey Gallo
Tommy Sinito
Joe Iacobacci
Russell Papalardo
Curly Montana

The Collinwood Group

Allie Calabrese
Tony Delguyd
Joe Bonarigo
John Del Zoppo
Jimmy Martino
Tony Occhionero
John Oliverio

Youngstown/Warren

Tony "Dope" Delsanter
   (deceased 1976)
Ronnie "Ronnie Crab" Carabbia
Charlie "Charlie Crab" Carabbia
   (missing, presumed dead)
Orlie "Orlie Crab" Carabbia
Joe Derose
   (missing, presumed dead)

Raymond Ferrito

• *The above men were alleged or reputed members, associate members, or associates of
the Cleveland Mafia. Sources include the Pennsylvania Crime Commission.*

THE PITTSBURGH COSA NOSTRA*
Circa 1984

Boss: John Sebastian LaRocca
Underboss: Joseph "Jo-Jo" Percora
Consigliere: Michael Genovese

Capos, Soldiers, and Associates

Gabriel "Kelly" Mannarino
Thomas Ciancutti
Charles Imburgia
Charles Porter
John Bazzano
Antonio Ripepi
Joseph Regino
Joseph Sica
Samuel J. Fashionatta
John C. Fontana
Michael Traficante
Henry Zottola

Youngstown/Warren, Ohio, Group

Vincent "Jimmy" Prato
Joey Naples
Lenine Strollo
Ernest Biondillo
Bernard Altshuller
Frank Lentine
Paul "Pinto" Holovatick
Peter Cascarelli

Altoona, Pennsylvania, Group

Alfred Corbo
Joseph Ruggiero
John Verilla
Victor Schiappa
Carl Venturato
John Caramadre
Vincent Caraciollo
Dennis Colello

• *The above men were alleged or reputed members, associate members, or associates of the Pittsburgh Mafia. Sources include the Pennsylvania Crime Commission.*

THE SOUTHERN CALIFORNIA COSA NOSTRA*

Circa 1985

Boss: Peter Milano
Underboss: Carmen Milano
Consigliere: Jack LoCicero

Capos

Mike Rizzitello
Vincent Caci
Luigi Gelfuso Jr.

Soldiers and Associates

Charles Cori
Stephen Cino
Rocco Zangari
Albert Nunez
Craig Fiato
Lawrence Fiato
John Demattia
John Vaccaro
Russell Masella

• *The above men were alleged or reputed members, associate members, or associates of the Southern California Mafia. Sources include the California Crime Commission and the Los Angeles Times.*

THE KANSAS CITY COSA NOSTRA*
Circa 1984

Bosses: Nick Civella
Carl "Cork" Civella
Underboss: Carl "Tuffy" Deluna
Consigliere: Unknown

Capos, Soldiers, Associates, and Others

Tony "Ripe" Civella
Peter Simone
Peter Tamburello
Charles Moretina
Tommy Lococo
Felix Ferina
Tommy Cacioppo
Willy Cammisano
Sam Ancona
Angelo Porrello

Las Vegas

Joe Agosto
Carl Thomas

• The above men were alleged or reputed members, associate members, or associates of the Kansas City, Missouri, Mafia. Sources include The Enforcer by Bill Roemer and the FBI.

WHAT HAPPENED TO THEM ALL?

Some of the players involved in La Cosa Nostra vanished without a trace. Others were caught and lived under scrutiny from that moment on.

Frank Brancato, partner in the Licatese faction of the Cleveland Mafia, was seventy-six when he died of natural causes in 1973.

Allie Calabrese died in prison in 1999 while serving a sentence for attempting to defraud a New Jersey bank.

John Calandra, Jack Licavoli's right-hand man, died of natural causes in 1992.

Ronnie "Ronnie Crab" Carabbia, Youngstown mobster convicted of killing Danny Greene, served almost twenty-three years in prison before being paroled in 2002.

Eugene "the Animal" Ciasullo, now in his sixties and semiretired, is perhaps the most successful of modern-day Cleveland Cosa Nostra figures. He has maintained a widely respected reputation nationwide while managing to serve minimal time in prison. He did spend two years in prison for a 1981 assault conviction. Ciasullo has two residences in Pennsylvania and spends winters at a third in Florida.

Pasquale "Butchie" Cisternino died in prison in 1990 of pancreatic cancer. He was fifty-six and left behind a wife and four children.

John DeMarco, boss of the Licatese faction of the Cleveland Cosa Nostra, died of a heart attack in 1972 at the age of sixty-eight. In his later years, he confined his mob activities to lending money on a short-term, high-interest basis.

Raymond Ferritto left WITSEC after only one year and lived in Pennsylvania. In 1992, he was convicted of criminal conspiracy and bookmaking charges. He served a short prison stint, was given three years' probation, and was ordered to pay $10,500 in fines. He retired to Florida in 2000 and died of congestive heart failure in 2004.

Jimmy "the Weasel" Fratianno died of Alzheimer's disease and a stroke in 1993. He was seventy-nine.

Joey Gallo, once heir apparent to the Cleveland Mafia throne, continues to serve a life sentence for drug racketeering.

Hartmut "the Surgeon" Graewe continues to serve a life sentence.

Joseph "Joe Loose" Iacobacci, an acknowledged member of La Cosa Nostra, was sentenced in 1996 to thirty months for his federal conviction in a scheme to defraud several New Jersey banks of $3 million. He has also served time for gambling and drug convictions. Iacobacci was released from his most recent prison sentence in 1998.

Tony Liberatore was released from prison in 1990 after serving eight years for racketeering. In 1993 he was convicted of money laundering and racketeering and sentenced to ten years. The conviction was upheld by the U.S. Supreme Court in 1995. Liberatore had appealed on the grounds that he suffered from Alzheimer's disease and thus was incompetent to stand trial. He died in prison in 1998.

James "Jack White" Licavoli died in prison in 1985. He was eighty-one.

Angelo "Big Ange" Lonardo was dropped from WITSEC around 1991 after moving back to northeast Ohio, an area obviously forbidden by the program. He lived quietly until his death in 2006 at the age of ninety-five.

Kevin McTaggart continues to serve a life sentence at the federal penitentiary in Terre Haute, Indiana. He is secretary of a Jaycees group made up of inmates. In 1989 he received a commendation for rushing to the aid of a female prison psychologist who had been stabbed by a disturbed inmate.

Anthony "the Old Man" Milano died in 1978 of natural causes. He was ninety.

Frank Milano died of natural causes in the sixties.

John "Curly" Montana served thirteen years in prison for his involvement in the 1981 kidnapping and murder of Chicago millionaire businessman Henry Podborny. In 2001, Montana, age eighty-two, was investigated for trying to sell a stolen painting worth $700,000. He was not charged and continues to reside in Cleveland.

Jackie Presser died of lung cancer in 1988 at the age of sixty-two.

Maishe Rockman was released from prison in 1993 for health reasons, after serving seven years of a twenty-one-year sentence imposed from his skimming case conviction. He died in 1995.

Tommy Sinito died of a heart attack in prison in 1997. He was fifty-nine. He was serving several concurrent sentences, including a seven- to twenty-five-year stint for the murder of mob associate and bodyguard David Perrier. Sinito's former attorney, Jim Willis, called him an honorable friend. "If he told you something, you could take it to the bank," Willis said. "He wasn't a crybaby like they put in jail today, calling you every five minutes collect, complaining about their sentence. He was from the old school."

Babe Triscaro died of a stroke in 1974.

Carmen Zagaria is out of WITSEC and living comfortably in an undisclosed location. He reportedly visits relatives in Cleveland.

MORE STORIES OF THE MAFIA

A HIGH-FLYING INFORMANT

By 1975, John Nardi's gambling habit was taking a toll. He was heavily in debt to several bookmakers, and Caesars Palace in Las Vegas was suing him over a $10,000 casino tab.

Through his connection to mob associate Dominick Bartone, Nardi fell into a drug smuggling scheme he thought might solve his financial problems. In 1959, Bartone was convicted in Miami for bribing customs agents and conspiring to ship arms and planes to anti-Castro forces in the Dominican Republic. Another interesting partner in the drug deal was Mitch WerBell, an international arms dealer from

Georgia. Reportedly, WerBell once worked for the C.I.A. Morton Franklin was the last principal. He was an insurance man and, along with Bartone, was implicated in the bankruptcy case of an Ohio bank.

Before the smuggling plan was executed, Florida investigators were on the move with indictments. Apparently they had a confidential informant:

> Report of Air Crash Investigation disclosed the decedent expired as the result of injuries sustained in an air crash which occurred in the Mojave desert at a location approximately 2 miles East of the Mojave Airport and approximately 1 mile north of State Route 58, Mojave, Rural, California . . . The events prior to the air crash would indicate the decedent was piloting a F-51-D Mustang . . . The decedent was flying Northbound toward the Mojave airport at about 5,000 feet. He indicated by radio that he was going down and run the pylons and implemented a slow down-ward roll. During the roll, he made the statement, "Oh, oh, no!", and

apparently applied power in an effort to pull out of the roll, however, he did not have enough altitude to recover and impacted the ground.

The decedent referred to in the report was Kenneth Burnstine, forty-three, of Fort Lauderdale, Florida. Burnstine was the pilot for the drug smuggling operation. As it turned out, Burnstine was the informant working with investigators. Despite the obvious suspicion, none of the Bartone smuggling ring members were officially connected with their pilot's sudden death.

THE WISDOM OF
TONY MILANO

In his eighties, Tony Milano was a dignified but lonely man who had lost most of his close friends to the average life expectancy. He had grayish-white hair, wore thick glasses, and was hard of hearing. A chain-smoker of Lucky Strikes, Milano attributed his longevity to a diet high in fruits and vegetables. He never drank water and professed to be his own doctor. Milano could often be found taking a casual walk in Little Italy, where he passed out candy to neighborhood kids.

His office was smoke-filled and lined with

bookcases. On a wall hung a picture of Abraham Lincoln. Next to that was a framed photograph of President Richard Nixon signed, "To Anthony Milano with best wishes." On his desk he kept a thermos of hot espresso that he brought fresh from home daily. Guests were served from white demitasse cups.

Milano was not one to grant interviews, but on occasion he spoke with *Cleveland Press* reporter Tony Natale or Mairy Jayn Woge of the *Cleveland Plain Dealer*. Naturally, they took the opportunity to ask about the M word, but Milano adamantly denied its existence.

"Mafia! Mafia! That's all I hear! The newspapers. The police. There is no such thing as the Mafia. Years ago when Italy was divided into states and rich barons ruled, there was a Mafia. It was started by bandits who stole from the rich. There is no such thing. Valachi? Baloney. He just told the government what it wanted to hear. And if the F.B.I. knows so much about it, why don't they get somebody into it. The only thing they're concerned about is the black list of Italians they want killed."

(Ironically, when Milano made that statement, a top secret plan was being readied by the F.B.I. to place a young undercover agent in the midst of the Bonanno Mafia family in New York. It was a phenomenally successful six-year operation.)

During Tony Milano's last years, he spent his time playing chess and recording his words of his wisdom in a pamphlet he titled *Philosophical Quotations by Anthony Milano*.

A sampling:

> Grace, courtesy and elegance are the arts that contribute to make life more pleasurable and beautiful.
> He who thinks he is so great, suddenly falls.
> Do everything you can, don't spend all you have, don't believe everything you hear and don't tell everything you know.
> In order to become dominator, it is necessary to give the people discipline, education, liberty and bread.
> If you want to live in peace, look, listen and be quiet.
> Study first the penal code, and then go swimming.
> The secret of power is desire.

YOUNGSTOWN: A HOT SPOT FOR ORGANIZED CRIME

"Organized crime [in Youngstown] is a lucrative business because of the sizeable mill-working population which provides a ready clientele for its services and goods," explained Cleveland strike force leader Steve Olah. "Add to that the political corruptibility, and it's a natural—almost like taking candy from a baby."

Former Youngstown attorney and San Francisco 49ers president Carmen Policy further added, "This is a working-class area and gambling is not considered a vice. In fact, gambling permeates everything. For its size, I admit, there is no city in America like Youngstown."

For decades, Sebastian "John" LaRocca was the Cosa Nostra boss who controlled the rackets in Pittsburgh, western Pennsylvania, and a section of the Mahoning Valley in Ohio. Gabriel "Kelly" Mannarino of New Kensington, Pennsylvania, rose through the ranks to become LaRocca's underboss. LaRocca, Mannarino, and Michael Genovese attended the famous 1957 Mafia conference in Appalachin, New York.

According to the F.B.I., part of the Pittsburgh-Cleveland conflict in Youngstown began in the sixties when Frank Brancato forced a successful Youngstown vending machine operator to cut the Cleveland family in for one-third of his profits. To ensure continued profits, Brancato had enforcers work to bring the vending man new customers. When the man's competitors became resentful, bombings and shootings followed.

It was after the damaging publicity of the bombing murder of Youngstown gangster Charlie Cavallaro and his eight-year-old son, and the maiming of another son, that both factions called a truce and agreed on territorial boundaries. Warren and Trumbull County, and Struthers in Mahoning County, went to Cleveland and was put under the control of Tony Delsanter and the Carabbia brothers. Youngstown and the rest of Mahoning County would be Pittsburgh territory, under the supervision of Jimmy Prato. The cease-fire and apportioning of turf stayed in effect until the late seventies.

Prato was known as "Briar-Hill Jimmy" after the old mill district that he grew up in. He was born in Calabria, Italy, and his uncle was reportedly one of the Youngstown area's earliest organized-crime bosses. Prato was a slight, balding man who spoke with a heavy Italian accent and attended church regularly. He was a powerful figure with influential connections. His attorney was Don Hanni, chairman of the Mahoning County Democratic Party and a member of the election board. For years, Prato had been investigated for running "the bug," a nickname for the local numbers game.

Prato's headquarters was his popular, neon-lit Calla-Mar Manor Restaurant, located near an Ohio turnpike interchange. There, behind closed doors, he conducted business meetings at the center table of the dining room. It was above this table that the F.B.I. was able, under federal Title III authority, to place a hidden listening device. When the roof began leaking from faulty installation of the bug, Prato's men discovered the hidden microphone and ripped it out. The F.B.I. agents listening from a nearby undercover vehicle immediately moved in to recover their expensive equipment. But for several tense hours, Prato refused to surrender the equipment and even had the audacity to order his security guard to arrest the F.B.I. agents for trespassing: the part-time security guard just happened to be the local police chief. He resigned as chief several days later.

Finally, additional agents were dispatched to the scene and surrounded the restaurant. They were instructed to arrest anyone causing an interference, while another agent was dispatched from Cleveland with a court order which was used to force the return of the F.B.I. equipment. When a reporter questioned Prato a few days later, he denied that the incident had occurred.

"I run a good business," he insisted. "I have a fine restaurant and banquet hall. No such thing happened in my place."

INDEX

RICK PORRELLO is chief of a suburban Cleveland police department. He is author of *The Rise and Fall of the Cleveland Mafia: Corn Sugar and Blood* (Barricade Books, 1995) and *Superthief: A Master Burglar, the Mafia and the Biggest Bank Heist in U.S. History* (Next Hat Press, 2006), winner of a *Foreword Magazine* True Crime award. Porrello began writing his first book during research into the murders of his grandfather and three uncles, Mafia leaders killed in Prohibition-era violence. He is an accomplished jazz drummer, having spent three years traveling worldwide with the late, great Sammy Davis Jr.